Longevity by Choice

THE ART OF RESETTING YOUR BODY

ZEN LEE

Zen Choice Publishing

Copyright ©

ISBN 978-1-7386096-8-0 (eBook)
ISBN 978-1-7386096-9-7 (hardcover)
ISBN 978-1-7386096-7-3 (paperback)
ISBN 978-1-7386096-6-6 (audiobook)

Contents

Table of Contents

Introduction

In today's world, we are exposed to a vast array of toxins and harmful elements in our daily routines, environment, and food. These toxins can accumulate in our bodies over time, leading to various health problems and reducing our overall quality of life. Moreover, the accumulation of toxins can help accelerate cellular aging and shorten our lifespan, forming a link between toxins and the aging process. What are toxins? Toxins are substances that are harmful to the body and can affect our health in many ways. These toxins come from both external (exogenous) sources, such as pollution, chemicals, and pesticides, and internal (endogenous) sources, such as histamine and uremic toxins.

While some substances produced by our own bodies, such as histamine, cortisol, glucose, and insulin, can benefit our bodies in the short term, the constant accumulation and long exposure of these can be toxic and harmful. Furthermore, we are constantly exposed to external toxic elements such as smoke, pollution, herbicides, pesticides, oxalates, parabens, BPA, PVC, phthalates, lead, and heavy metals. We may be exposed to specific toxins that can harm our bodies depending on our lifestyle, community, and location.

By resetting our bodies, we can eradicate these toxins and harmful elements to improve our health and prevent diseases. Resetting, detoxing, and cleansing our bodies entail eliminating harmful toxins and substances that have built up over time. Longevity by Choice: The Art of Resetting Your Body is a comprehensive guidebook designed to equip you with the knowledge and tools required to detoxify and cleanse your body from both endogenous and exogenous toxins to achieve optimal health and longevity.

In this book, you will learn the different types of toxins that affect our bodies, how they impact our health, and the steps you can take to reset your body and eliminate them. We will give you examples of toxins that enter our bodies based on where you live, your lifestyle, and your profession. By doing so, you will gain an in-depth understanding of how these processes work and their significance in promoting a healthier body.

Each chapter will focus on a different organ or system in the body, starting with the respiratory system and moving onto the digestive system, skin, and other systems affected by toxins, describing the toxins that can build up in that organ, the damage they can cause, and the symptoms that indicate a need for cleansing. For example, depending on your work and lifestyle, your lungs may be exposed to toxins such as smoke, pollution, fiberglass, and paint, while herbicides, pesticides, and cleaning chemicals can be harmful for the skin. Heavy metals can also affect these organs. We will also go over how harmful elements can build up in the brain, liver, kidneys, and other vital organs, causing headaches, fatigue, and digestive problems.

To provide you with actionable steps, in each chapter, we will explore a variety of detox approaches to suit different needs and lifestyles. Whether you're looking for an intensive, short-term cleanse or simple ways to boost your daily detox, you'll find an array of options here. These options will be based on scientific studies or medical advice that supports cleansing. In addition, we will provide general information on which diets and populations are more likely to suffer from organ dysfunction caused by toxins. It is critical to understand when your body requires assistance, how frequently cleansing is advised by doctors, and what to expect after cleansing.

Throughout this book, we will prioritize natural, easier, non-GMO, organic, and affordable options as much as possible. Natural supplement choices will be included, though specific brands won't be mentioned. Instead, these supplements can be accessed on our website, www.longevitybychoice.com, where you'll also have the opportunity to claim a **free bonus**, access online courses, receive discount codes for upcoming book series, and explore an array of additional free resources.

By the end of this book, you will have gained the knowledge and tools you need to cleanse your body, reduce the risk of health problems caused by toxins, and reset your body to a healthier state. Whether you are seeking an in-depth detox or simple ways to incorporate cleansing into your daily routine, Longevity by Choice: The Art of Resetting Your Body will guide you on your journey to a happier and healthier you. So, let's get started on the art of resetting your body!

Chapter 1

RESETTING THE BRAIN

Have you ever encountered cognitive difficulties, such as trouble concentrating or a sense that your cognitive function is not at its optimal level? You are not alone. In our fast-paced modern world, mental fatigue has become an epidemic. The non-stop stimuli of work, technology, and social obligations put immense pressure on our brains. Concentration falters, cognition feels hampered, and focus flees from our grasp. The mind's grasp on clarity loosens. The accumulation of both endogenous and exogenous toxins in our brain can have a significant impact on our ability to concentrate and focus, making it challenging to complete tasks effectively.

Yet solutions exist to renew the mind and body. By making brain health a priority, we can destress and detoxify our neural pathways back to peak performance. After all, the brain is the command center for the body's functions. Clear the clutter, and cognition comes easier. Adopt brain-benefiting habits, and thinking becomes fluid again. With consistent care, we can rediscover mental clarity and overcome the challenges of a toxic world. A detoxed mind sustains focus amidst the chaos.

This chapter will give an overview of the most common toxins and harmful elements that affect our brain, along with the symptoms they cause and how they can enter our brain. We will also discuss how different communities deal with this issue and how we can take control of our brain health by developing stronger willpower. The chapter will address how detoxifying, primarily through prevention, could contribute to keeping our brain healthy, in addition to some natural remedies that can be used to support brain function.

There are several toxins and harmful elements that have an impact on the brain, and they can enter our brain through a variety of pathways, including the blood-brain barrier, cranial bones, and ears. We will identify the most common toxins and harmful elements, such as histamine, urea, and melatonin imbalance caused by screen exposure, smoking, alcohol, and medications, as well as the less common toxins, such as cortisol, dopamine, serotonin, and oxytocin effects, high-frequency radiation exposure, and low-frequency radiation exposure.

Environmental toxins can inflict far-reaching damage, especially on our vulnerable brains. This chapter will explore common symptoms of toxic exposure, like brain fog, memory loss, anxiety, and depression. We'll examine the science behind these cognitive and psychological effects. Beyond mental impacts, we'll also discuss how toxins harm overall health by impairing the immune system, disrupting hormones, and potentially contributing to disease. Understanding these insidious consequences is the first step toward reclaiming well-being.

To regain control of our brain health, we must first understand the impact of toxins and then investigate various detoxification methods. We will explore the benefits of boosting happiness neurotransmitters, optimizing the gut microbiome, and strengthening gut brain communication. Moreover, we will discuss the benefits of HIIT (High-Intensity Interval Training) exercises, self-hypnosis, and deep habit eradication.

In addition, the chapter will look at how to form new neuronal connections and introduce some herbal or natural remedies that can help with brain function, including Ginkgo, Danggui Shaoyao San, Lion Melen, Bacopa, Tyrosine amino acid, Creatine, Copper, B6 vitamin, Vitamin B12, Vitamin D3, Iron, Magnesium L-threonate, Omega3, Choline, Potassium, and electrolytes. Additionally, we will also examine how electromagnetic frequencies, from cellular signals to wireless technologies, can influence neural function for better or worse. We will also investigate the link between smoking and the brain, the role of microbiomes in the brain, and the relationship between neurotransmitters and mood.

This chapter will provide you with insights into the importance of resetting our brain, which can contribute to a much healthier and more fulfilling life, especially as we age. By improving our cognitive function, enhancing our mental health, and improving our overall well-being, can lead to better aging and a more satisfying life as we grow older. While some of these topics will be covered in greater depth in subsequent books in the "Longevity by Choice" series, this chapter will provide you with an overview to help you understand how to reset your brain and improve your overall health.

Understanding the Impact of Toxins and Harmful Elements on the Brain

The brain is one of the most complex and delicate organs in the body, controlling all bodily functions and processes, but its complexity renders it susceptible to harm. Toxins can infiltrate through numerous pathways, disrupting neural function and mental clarity, such as:

- Blood-Brain Barrier: This protective interface blocks toxins from entering the brain, but some sneak through, like alcohol and certain drugs. These substances infiltrate delicate neural networks, inflicting damage that degrades cognition.

- Cranial Bone: Harmful rays such as X-rays can penetrate the cranial bone, carrying toxins directly into the brain's delicate networks. This exposure can elicit mild neurological symptoms like headaches and vertigo or more severe symptoms like radiation sickness and brain cancer.

- Gamma Rays: Gamma rays readily infiltrate tissues and bones due to their intense photon energy. Large exposures can inflict grave harm on the vulnerable brain and other organs.

- Neutrons: These subatomic particles readily bypass physical barriers like bone to reach and disrupt cerebral structures. Neutron infiltration can severely impair neural function, though most exposure occurs in nuclear or clinical settings.

- Ear: Loud noise damages inner ear structures, enabling toxin trespass and leading to hearing impairment and other auditory issues. In addition, there are specific types of chemicals, such as solvents and pesticides, that can infiltrate the body through the ear canal, causing harm to the brain and its functions.

- Nose (Olfactory Pathway): Within the nasal cavity, airborne chemicals interact with delicate olfactory cells. Gases and vapors that we inhale interact with our olfactory receptor cells. These signals are subsequently sent from the olfactory nerve fibers towards the brain-connected olfactory bulbs. The blood-brain barrier, which generally prohibits chemicals from accessing the brain down this route, prevents the olfactory pathway from having immediate entry into deeper brain structures. However, some airborne contaminants, including viruses or toxins, can get through this barrier. In these circumstances, they might be harmful if they penetrate deeper brain regions.

- Eyes (Optic Nerve): Chemicals often do not enter the brain through the eyes. The optic nerve transmits vision signals as opposed to allowing chemicals to enter the brain as it transfers visual information from your eyes to the brain. It's important to keep in mind, though, that specific irritants or toxins might impact the eyes and produce inflammation, irritation, or vision issues. Potential consequences that indirectly influence the brain can result from major eye damage or infection spreading to the surrounding tissues.

Understanding the various pathways by which toxins can enter the brain is critical for developing methods to minimize exposure and prevent the adverse repercussions of these substances on the brain.

Common Toxins and Harmful Elements That Affect Our Brain

Toxins and harmful elements can have a detrimental effect on the brain's well-being, resulting in a wide range of cognitive and neurological disorders. The following are some of the most common toxins and harmful elements that affect the brain:

- Histamine: Histamine is a chemical that the body's immune system produces as a reaction to an allergen. An excessive amount of histamine, on the other hand, can cause a variety of neurological and cognitive disorders, such as memory decline and disorientation.

- Insulin: Insulin is a hormone that serves to control how our bodies use glucose. Unbalanced insulin levels can result in high blood sugar levels, which, as time passes, could damage our nerves and cognitive function.

- Pesticides: Some pesticides contain known neurotoxic compounds that might interfere with brain function and perhaps contribute to the emergence of illnesses. According to studies, chronic exposure to these chemicals is linked to diseases including Parkinson's and Alzheimer's.

- Solvents: The nervous system and cognitive functioning can be affected by breathing in or being exposed for a prolonged amount of time to solvents such as paint thinners and cleaning chemicals. This may lead to problems with memory retention and difficulties with concentration and attention.

- Arsenic: Long-term exposure to arsenic through contaminated water or certain foods has been linked to memory impairments and deficits.

- Carbon monoxide: Inhaling carbon monoxide from heating systems or exhaust fumes can impair brain function by limiting oxygen to the brain.

- Manganese: High levels of manganese exposure, particularly occupational exposure, can cause Parkinson's-like symptoms such as tremors and difficulty moving.

- Air pollution: High levels of air pollution, particularly in cities, have been scientifically linked to cognitive impairment, memory loss, and Alzheimer's disease.

- Lead (Pb): Lead is a metal that poses serious risks to our nervous system and brain. Exposure to lead, which is commonly present in paints, water pipes, and contaminated soil, has been linked to deficits, particularly in children.

- Mercury (Hg): Mercury poisoning, particularly from mercury-contaminated seafood or dental fillings, may result in dementia, tremors, irritability, and damage to the central nervous system.

- Medications: Certain medications, which include benzodiazepines, anticholinergics, and antipsychotics, are capable of resulting in cognitive and neurological complications such as disorientation, memory loss, and dizziness.

- Methamphetamine (Meth): Methamphetamine, also called "meth," is an extremely potent stimulant with significant neurological effects. It may result in cardiovascular issues, memory loss, functional and structural modifications to the brain, and significant long-term neurological damage.

- Smoking and Alcohol: Both smoking and drinking alcohol can cause significant brain damage, including shrinking the cerebral cortex in the brain, a region responsible for brain function.

- Melatonin imbalance: Melatonin is a hormonal substance that manages our sleep-wake cycle. Exposure to blue-light-emitting screens, such as computers and smartphones, can interfere with the body's natural melatonin production, causing insomnia along with other sleep disorders.

- Urea: Urea is a waste product generated by the liver during the protein breakdown process. Excess urea in the bloodstream can cause a wide range of cognitive symptoms, including disorientation, foggy thinking, and dementia.

Less Common Toxins and Harmful Elements That Affect Our Brain

In addition to the most common toxins, several less common toxins and harmful elements can have adverse impacts on brain health. Some of these include:

- Cortisol: Cortisol is a hormonal substance that the body produces in reaction to stress. Cortisol levels that are constantly too high can cause cognitive symptoms such as forgetfulness and difficulty concentrating.

- Dopamine/serotonin/oxytocin: Dopamine, serotonin, and oxytocin are neurotransmitters that regulate mood, social bonding, and pleasure. However, imbalances in these neurotransmitters can cause anxiety, mood swings, and depression, along with other cognitive and neurological symptoms.

- High-frequency radiation: High-frequency radiation from mobile devices and Wi-Fi routers, for example, can cause dizziness, headaches, and various other cognitive symptoms.

- Low-frequency radiation exposure: Low-frequency radiation from transmission lines and electrical devices may result in depressive disorders, fatigue, and various other mental health issues.

- PCBs: Polychlorinated biphenyls (PCBs) exposure, particularly through contaminated seafood or other food sources, can cause delays in development, cognitive and behavioral issues, and cancer.

What Are the Most Common Symptoms Toxins and Harmful Elements Produce?

The symptoms associated with toxin and harmful element exposure vary depending on a variety of factors, including the type and level of exposure, as well as individual characteristics such as age, health status, and genetics. However, some of the most common symptoms associated with exposure to these toxins are as follows:

- Headaches and migraines

- Fatigue and weakness

- Memory and cognitive problems

- Mood changes and depression

- Dizziness and vertigo

- Nausea and vomiting

- Respiratory difficulties

- Skin irritation and rashes

- Muscle pain and weakness

- Digestive problems

- Vision and hearing impairments

- Cardiovascular issues

It is worth noting that these symptoms of toxin exposure can mimic those of other health conditions. As a result, if you experience any symptoms after being exposed to toxins or harmful elements, you must seek medical attention. Moreover, it is also important to note that these symptoms may appear immediately after exposure or may take longer to develop, and some people may be more sensitive to the effects of these toxins and harmful elements than others.

Take Control and Build Willpower for a Healthier Brain

As we get older, our brain's health and functioning can decline due to various factors, including exposure to toxins and other harmful substances. Despite this, there are measures we can implement to sustain and even enhance our brain health through specific actions and practices. An effective approach is to prioritize prevention through detoxification, which may entail avoiding toxins and harmful substances while also supporting the body's natural detoxification mechanisms. Avoiding smoking and excessive alcohol consumption, using organic and natural products whenever possible, and limiting exposure to environmental pollutants are also examples of ways to do so.

Research findings have shown that being exposed to toxins and other harmful substances can accelerate aging and cause cognitive decline. Detoxification can help slow this process down and improve over-all brain health. A healthy diet, regular exercise, and stress management techniques are all ways to help the body's natural detoxification process.

In addition to detoxification, building willpower can help improve brain health. Willpower is the ability to resist temptation and postpone gratification, which is vital to sustaining healthy habits and avoiding unhealthy behaviors. Pleasure hormones, like dopamine and serotonin, are produced by the brain and have an impact on mood and motivation regulation. These hormones are produced by different organs in the body, including the brain and the gut, and can be impacted by various factors like diet and exercise, spending time in nature, and socializing.

To increase happiness neurotransmitters, improve gut flora, and improve the connection between the intestine and the brain, it is helpful to focus on improving the health of our gut microbiome. Research has found a correlation between the gut microbiome and brain health, indicating that supporting the health of the gut may have a positive impact on cognitive function and overall well-being. The brain influences how the intestines work, particularly how functional immune cells perform. Similarly, the gut has an influence on emotions, thought processes, and mental health. To maintain the health of the gut microbiome, it may be helpful to consume a diet that is both nutritious and diverse, incorporating probiotics or prebiotics. Additionally, avoiding exposure to harmful toxins can help prevent disruption of the gut microbiome. These are all potential ways to support gut health and enhance a balanced microbiome.

Another approach to building willpower is to establish routine and perseverance by incorporating regular exercise, such as high-intensity interval training (HIIT) exercises. These types of exercises have been shown to have numerous benefits that not only improve physical fitness but also reduce stress, improve cognitive function by increasing neurotrophic factors, and enhance brain plasticity.

In addition, it is critical to be mindful of our habits and work on eliminating bad habits that may be harmful to our brain health. This can entail recognizing when our inner voice is not helping us and developing strategies for dealing with negative self-talk. Self-hypnosis can be an effective tool in this situation, but it is still a topic that many people are unfamiliar with. However, it is gaining acceptance as a medical treatment option for a variety of conditions. Meditation, yoga, and deep breathing exercises can also assist with stress reduction and promote relaxation, which could ultimately lead to better willpower and healthier brain function.

Finally, creating new neuronal connections through neuronal plasticity is another important aspect of developing willpower and enhancing overall brain function. Neuronal plasticity is a term used to describe the brain's capacity to form new pathways and connections as a result of learning and experience. One way to promote neuronal plasticity is by engaging in activities that challenge the brain, which is called neurofeedback. It is a technique that helps train the brain to operate more efficiently. Activities such as learning a new skill or language, playing a musical instrument, or engaging in any other creative endeavor are examples of ways to enhance cognitive function and promote the creation of new neuronal connections.

Overall, taking control of your health and building willpower are crucial steps to undertake in enhancing brain health and preventing cognitive decline for a healthier life. It is important to remember that incorporating healthy habits and detoxing the brain are ongoing processes that require time and effort. However, the benefits of doing so are immense, particularly in terms of maintaining a healthy brain as we age. These topics will be explored in greater detail in the third book of the "Longevity by Choice" series.

Use of Natural Remedies

In the pursuit of a healthier brain, it is important to include the use of natural remedies that have been proven to improve brain function. For centuries, natural remedies have been used to improve a wide range of medical conditions, including brain health. Among the natural remedies that could be beneficial for brain health are:

1. Ginkgo: Ginkgo is an herb that has been used for thousands of years in traditional Chinese medicine. It is believed to enhance cognition by increasing blood flow and oxygenation to the brain. According to studies, taking 12–240 mg of ginkgo per day can improve blood flow to the brain, which can enhance memory and concentration and reduce the risk of age-related cognitive decline. It is advisable to consult with a healthcare professional before starting any new supplements to ensure safety.

2. Danggui Shaoyao San (DSS): DSS is anoth-

er natural remedy that has been discovered to improve irrigation in the central nervous system (CNS). This natural remedy is made up of several Chinese herbs, including Angelica sinensis and Paeonia lactiflora. DSS has been shown to be especially effective in improving blood flow to the brain and lowering the risk of stroke in patients. DSS has been shown in studies to improve cognitive function in people with Alzheimer's disease, highlighting its potential as a therapeutic treatment for the disease.

3. Lion's Mane: This is a mushroom that has been found to increase the production of Nerve Growth Factor (NGF), a protein necessary for the development and maintenance of neurons that may help reduce brain inflammation. It also contains compounds that can increase the production of melanin, a pigment essential for neuronal health and function.

4. Bacopa: Bacopa monniera is an herbal supplement that has been used in ancient Ayurvedic medicine to treat many ailments for centuries. Studies have shown that bacopa helps improve cognitive function, memory, and concentration. It is known to contain bacosides that protect the brain from oxida-

tive stress and improve intercellular communication.

5. Tyrosine, Copper, and Vitamin B6: Tyrosine is an amino acid that is required for the synthesis of dopamine, the reward hormone, a neurotransmitter that is important for motivation and pleasure, and thus indirectly aids in the development of good habits and overcoming addiction. Copper and vitamin B6 are also required for dopamine production and can help improve mood, reduce stress, and improve cognitive function.

6. B complex & Magnesium Bisglycinate, and Magnesium Threonate: B-complex vitamins and magnesium are both required for proper brain and nervous system function. B-complex vitamins can help with stress reduction, mood enhancement, and cognitive function. Magnesium, especially magnesium bisglycinate and magnesium threonate, can contribute to better brain function and lower the risk of cognitive decline. Magnesium bisglycinate is quickly absorbed by the body, and it can aid in relaxation, whereas magnesium threonate is believed to improve cognitive abilities and memory.

7. Choline: Choline is crucial for the production of neurotransmitters and the formation

of the membranes of brain cells, making it necessary for maintaining brain health. It promotes learning, memory, and cognitive function.

8. Vitamin D3: Vitamin D3 is essential for maintaining cognitive and mental health. It promotes the development and functioning of brain cells and may act as a defense against neurodegenerative illnesses.

9. Omega-3: Omega-3 fatty acids are good for your brain since they are vital elements of brain cell membranes and have a role in neurotransmission. They may lower your likelihood of developing neurodegenerative illnesses and are linked to enhanced cognitive performance.

10. Iron and Electrolytes: Iron is involved in the production of hemoglobin (red blood cells); it carries oxygen to the brain. Inadequate iron levels in the human body can cause cognitive impairment and memory issues. Electrolytes, on the other hand, such as potassium and sodium, are vital to maintaining adequate hydration and balance in the human body, which is essential to healthy brain function.

11. Supplements that Reduce Stress and Ox-

idative Stress: Supplements include ashwagandha, passionflower, rhodiola, lavender, green tea, berries, and grape extract (resveratrol). These supplements offer stress-relieving qualities and can help fight oxidative stress in the brain, supporting general cognitive health.

12. Probiotics for Brain Health: Certain probiotic strains like Bacillus subtilis, Lactobacillus helveticus, Lactobacillus rhamnosus, Bifidobacterium bifidum, subtilis, breve, infant, and longum have demonstrated beneficial effects on brain health and cognitive performance. They might help regulate mood and lessen brain inflammation.

13. Maca: A plant-based product with prospective benefits for brain health is maca. Despite the paucity of evidence, several studies imply that it may improve mood and cognitive function.

14. Nicotinamide Adenine Dinucleotide (NAD): NAD, or nicotinamide adenine dinucleotide, is a coenzyme that is considered necessary in the production of cellular energy in the mitochondria. Mitochondria are known to be the powerhouses of cells. Supplementing with NAD precursors can help to maintain or increase NAD+ levels, which can de-

cline with age and result in mitochondrial dysfunction. This is especially advantageous for the brain, which needs a lot of energy to perform diverse cognitive tasks such as decision-making and the formation of new habits. NAD indirectly increases energy levels, improving the effectiveness and efficiency of key brain functions.

15. Glutathione and Milk Thistle: Glutathione is a powerful antioxidant that is required for detoxification and brain protection from the effects of oxidative stress and damage. It is usually given as an injection, but it also exists in supplements or in foods that contain glutathione. Milk thistle is an herb that has been shown to regulate liver function while enhancing the body's capacity to detoxify.

In addition to these supplements, there are other natural remedies that can help improve brain irrigation and oxygenation, both of which are necessary for maintaining a healthy brain. Moreover, the development of a new network of vessels is necessary for the production of new neurons and neural connections, which play a vital role in supporting brain health and function as well as promoting neurogenesis and brain plasticity. Among these remedies are:

1. Ruscus aculeatus, Rusco extract: Research has found that these herbs enhance blood

circulation.

2. Horse Chestnut (cortex, leaves, seed): These herbs have been shown to increase circulation and decrease inflammation, both of which may improve brain health.

3. Ginkgo Biloba leaves: As previously stated, Ginkgo Biloba is known for its ability to improve blood circulation to the brain.

Finally, the importance of sleep for the health of the brain should not be overlooked. In fact, sleep habits have been extensively addressed in Book 1 of the "Longevity by Choice" series. Melatonin is created during sleep, and it helps regulate the circadian cycle and hormone balance. Focusing on good sleep habits, creating a relaxing sleep environment, avoiding screens before bed, and adhering to a regular sleep schedule can be helpful for cognitive function, memory consolidation, and overall brain health. Natural remedies and nutrients, combined with healthy sleeping habits, regular exercise, and reduced exposure to harmful environmental toxins, can help promote the brain's overall wellness while boosting cognitive function.

Chapter 2

LIVER CLEANSE

As we grow older, our organs weaken in efficiency, and our body's capacity to get rid of pollutants decreases. In particular, the liver is in charge of cleansing the body and dissolving toxic substances, yet it is susceptible to stress and toxic overload. As a result, it is critical to consider ways to eliminate the highest number of toxins from our bodies as we age. This involves adding liver cleansing, also known as hepatic detoxification, to our health and longevity regimen.

The liver is a critical organ that conducts numerous processes, such as generating bile, breaking down lipids, and preserving vital nutrients. However, lifestyle decisions and dietary practices can result in a high level of toxins that overwork the liver and decrease its effectiveness. When liver health is neglected, toxins or fat can accumulate, which can cause malfunctions and other symptoms that may affect our general health and longevity.

A liver cleanse can assist in removing toxic accumulation and improving liver function. In this portion of the book, we will look at the health advantages of liver cleansing for the lifespan, including how to reverse processes like fatty liver. We're also going to talk about how important it is to undergo a liver cleanse before beginning intensive diets like ketogenic, OMAD, or other similar diets, as well as during candida and parasite eradication strategies.

Even though the liver and several additional organs within our body have mechanisms for getting rid of toxins, the significant quantities of toxins that we experience today far surpass their ability to eliminate them. Without our assistance, our bodies cannot properly clear toxic substances, more so as we age. As a consequence, it is essential to assist our systems in successfully eliminating toxins in order to enhance the functioning of the liver and maximize longevity.

The goal of this chapter is to provide you with the expertise and information you need to grasp the value of liver cleansing for longevity and include it in your overall wellness and longevity strategy. By implementing efforts to promote our liver's health, we can guarantee that each of our organs operates properly and that we relish good health throughout our lives.

Signs of an Unhealthy Liver

The liver is an important organ that processes nutrition, detoxifies toxic chemicals, and produces bile. When the liver is not performing well, it can cause a variety of liver dysfunctions, such as fatty liver, liver toxicity, and hepatitis. Listed below are a few of the most frequently observed symptoms of liver disease:

1. Jaundice: Jaundice is a common indication of liver failure, especially if the liver is unable to flush bilirubin from the blood. This substance is a yellow pigment that is formed when red blood cells degrade. It can produce skin and eye yellowing, black urine, and pale feces.

2. Fatigue: Fatigue is another prevalent symptom of liver failure, especially in those with hepatitis and chronic fatty liver disease. As the liver deteriorates, it may be unable to break down nutrients and produce energy, resulting in fatigue.

3. Abdominal pain and swelling: In cases of liver disease, especially if the liver is enlarged, ab-

dominal discomfort and swelling can occur. This might cause pain and soreness in the top right quadrant of the abdomen.

4. Nausea and vomiting: Nausea and vomiting can develop in conditions of liver malfunction, especially when the body's liver is unable to properly process toxins. This can cause feelings of being lightheaded, throwing up, and a loss of appetite.

5. High cholesterol levels: High levels of cholesterol can develop as a result of bile duct obstruction, which causes the liver to generate less bile. This can cause cholesterol to build up in the blood, leading to elevated cholesterol levels.

6. Easy bruising and bleeding: In cases of liver malfunction, easy bruising and bleeding may develop, especially if the liver's function fails to produce adequate clotting factors, which leads to easy bruising and excessive bleeding.

7. Mental confusion: Liver disease, particularly liver failure, can result in mental disorientation, resulting in confusion, cognitive impairment, a lack of sleep, and forgetfulness.

If you encounter any of the above symptoms, you should seek medical assistance immediately because they could suggest liver dysfunction. Early detection and therapy can help avoid additional liver damage and improve the health of the liver. Adopting a healthy lifestyle, including a balanced diet, frequent exercise, and avoiding high alcohol intake, is also important for promoting liver health and preventing liver disease.

Diets, Habits, or Substances That Rapidly Produce This Liver Dysfunctions

The liver is a vital organ that detoxifies the body and breaks down harmful toxins. Diets, habits, or substances that are harmful to the liver's health, on the other hand, can result in liver dysfunction and major health concerns.

A high-fructose diet is one of the most significant reasons. Studies have demonstrated that high-fructose diets, such as those containing high-fructose corn syrup, may result in fatty liver disease. This is due to the liver's conversion of fructose into fat, which can build up and cause harm to the liver over time.

High-fat diets are another type of diet that might damage the liver. This is due to the fact that excess fat may build up in the liver, causing inflammation and harm. The ensuing illness, which is called non-alcoholic fatty liver disease (NAFLD), grows more frequent and, if left untreated, can progress to more serious liver damage.

Alcoholism is also one of the leading causes of liver dysfunction, which can lead to liver failure and cirrhosis. People who have a history of drinking alcohol regularly are more likely to suffer liver damage, even from moderate alcohol consumption.

There are several less well-known habits and substances that might cause liver disease in addition to these well-known causes. For example, large doses of some drugs or supplements, as well as exposure to environmental pollutants and certain illnesses, can be damaging to the liver.

It is of the utmost importance that you remain aware of these potential risks and take precautions to protect the health of your liver. This involves choosing a diet that has low fast-digesting carbs, like sugar and refined carbs, while also following a low-bad-fat approach focusing on monounsaturated fats and boosting the intake of healthy slow-digesting carbs and necessary polyunsaturated fats. Limit alcohol consumption and stay away from harmful substances. By implementing these steps, you may help guarantee that the liver stays healthy and operates effectively in the future, lowering your chance of significant health problems.

Secondary Effects

There are several secondary effects that might arise from the liver's dysfunction, all of which must be carefully taken into account. A prime instance of this is the liver's function of removing hormones from the circulation that have served their intended purpose. If these hormones linger in the body for an extended amount of time, they can cause major problems such as glucose resistance, hormone imbalances, and chronic stress. This emphasizes the critical need for a functioning liver in order to achieve good overall health.

Another important function of the liver is assimilation and fat digestion. Among other things, the liver is in charge of lipid, good fat, omega-3, and liposomal vitamin absorption. When the liver isn't working effectively, the absorption of all these essential nutrients suffers, resulting in a slew of health issues. To ensure optimal nutritional absorption and general health, it is critical to sustain a healthy liver through a suitable diet and lifestyle practices.

How Do You Know if Your Liver Is Not Removing the Toxins?

There are various symptoms that may be indicative of liver dysfunction when the liver fails to eliminate toxins effectively. These symptoms, which may vary between acute and/or chronic, should not be disregarded because they might lead to major health concerns. Some of the acute signs that your liver may be struggling include:

- Chronic fatigue, sluggishness, and tiredness.

- White or yellow-coated tongue and bad breath.

- Unexpected weight gain, especially around the abdomen.

- Cravings and/or blood sugar issues.

- Painful headaches and poor digestion.

- Nauseous after eating fatty meals.

Prevention Is the Key

Prevention is vital for maintaining a healthy, functioning liver. We are able to reduce our likelihood of liver dysfunction while maintaining good liver function by implementing healthy lifestyle practices. Among the effective preventive measures are:

1. Maintaining a healthy weight by having a balanced diet and exercising regularly.

2. Eliminating high-sugar, high-fat diets, which can contribute to fatty liver disease.

3. Reducing or entirely avoiding alcohol consumption.

4. Avoiding exposure to hazardous chemicals and toxins in the workplace and environment.

5. Getting a hepatitis A and B vaccine assists in reducing the chance of infection.

6. Abiding by prescription guidelines and abstaining from the use of recreational drugs.

7. Employing precautions during sexual activity in order to reduce the risk of contracting hepatitis B and C.

List of Harmful Substances to the Liver

There are several substances that could harm the liver, including:

- Refined foods

- Chronic malnutrition

- Fried foods

- Canned foods and foods cooked with aluminum foil

- Margarines

- Alcohol

- High-fructose diet

- Saturated fats and trans fats

- Diets deficient in methionine and choline
  (predisposition to fatty liver, cirrhosis, cancer, and other diseases)

- Consumption of bad fats

- High fructose corn syrup

- Eating uncooked shellfish

- Some medications (including acetaminophen)

- Eating poisonous wild mushrooms

- Chronic hepatitis B

- Exposure to chemicals, PVC, BPA, and heavy
  metals (such as mercury)

- Additives, colorants, and preservatives to
  avoid

- Parabens

Habits That Help Liver Purification in the Daily Routine

The liver is an essential organ that performs numerous functions in the human body, particularly

detoxification and blood purification. As a result, it is critical to maintain the liver's health through good practices that support liver function. Here are some daily routines that can aid with liver purification:

1. Stay Hydrated: Drinking sufficient water is vital for liver well-being since it helps drain toxins out of the body. Try drinking a minimum of eight to ten glasses of water per day.

2. Limit alcohol consumption: Drinking excessively can be harmful to liver health since it causes damage and inflammation to the cells inside the liver. If you do drink alcohol, restrict your consumption and enjoy it moderately.

3. Regular exercise: Regular exercise has been demonstrated to contribute to better liver function by reducing inflammation and promoting healthy blood flow. Include a minimum of thirty minutes of physical exercise into your normal daily routine.

4. Eat a Balanced Diet: A diet high in nutritious foods, fruits, and vegetables supplies the liver with the nutrients it requires to function properly. Incorporate antioxidant-rich foods such as grapefruit, green tea, and garlic into your diet.

5. Get Enough Sleep: Sleeping is extremely

important for liver health since the liver cleanses your body throughout the night. Opt for at least seven to eight hours of good sleep every night to provide the liver with the rest that it requires.

6. Toxin Avoidance: Limit your exposure to environmental toxins such as chemicals, pesticides, and heavy metals. In addition, eliminate refined foods, sweetened beverages, and fast food because these might increase the liver's workload.

Incorporating these practices into your daily life may assist in liver purification as well as improve your general well-being.

Substances That Help Keep the Liver Healthy and Eliminate Its Free Radicals

A number of substances have been observed that promote the proper function of the liver's cells and aid in the removal of toxic free radicals. The substances in question include cruciferous veggies, citrus fruit, apple cider vinegar, natural vegetable juices, dandelions, milk thistle, other high-potassium meals, raw garlic, turmeric, and carrots.

Cruciferous vegetables like kale, broccoli, and Brussels sprouts are believed to hold compounds that play a role in the liver's detoxification and inflammation reduction. Lemon is very rich in vitamin C, a potent antioxidant that protects the liver's tissues from oxidative damage. Animal studies have demonstrated that apple cider vinegar improves liver function and reduces inflammation. Raw vegetable juices, specifically beet and carrot juices, have been shown to boost liver function and minimize fat accumulation in the liver.

Dandelion has been widely used as a natural cure for liver diseases, and new research indicates that its consumption could boost liver function by lowering inflammation and reducing oxidative stress. Milk thistle is a well-known herbal remedy that has been found to help protect the liver against toxicity and reduce inflammation. Consuming foods such as sweet potatoes, avocado, spinach, and bananas, which are high in potassium, may help mitigate the likelihood of developing liver disease.

Turmeric, an Indian spice, includes an organic compound known as curcumin that has been shown to protect the liver against toxicity and reduce inflammation. Carrots have beta-carotene, a potent antioxidant linked to a lower likelihood of liver cancer. Raw garlic has substances that are beneficial for liver detoxification and inflammation reduction.

Integrating any of these foods into your daily diet can be an effective method to preserve liver health and reduce your risk of developing liver disease.

However, before making any modifications to your meals or starting a new diet, it is important to check with a healthcare expert.

How to Ingest Them, How Often, and When

Here are some guidelines for when and how often to consume the substances that help maintain your liver's functioning properly and eliminate free radicals:

- Digestive Juice Cleanse: Starting your day with a glass of freshly squeezed organic raw celery juice that includes insoluble fiber and filtered water is an excellent way to kickstart your day. One tablespoon of lemon juice and one tablespoon of extra-virgin olive oil can be added to this juice to make it more flavorful. This combination of ingredients helps in liver cleansing, increases bile production, and supports digestion function.

- Detox Tea: Throughout the day, consider noshing on dried berries and nuts while sipping on black or green tea infused with turmeric, ginger, and lemon, which can be a beneficial way to support liver health. This tea blend has anti-inflammatory qualities and may assist in the reduction of oxidative stress in the liver.

- Meals: Include meals that are rich in choline and methionine to stimulate the use of fat that is stored within the liver as an energy source, mobilizing this fat out of the liver for cleansing. Examples of such foods include eggs, potatoes, some dairy products, cruciferous vegetables (broccoli, Brussels sprouts, and cauliflower), certain types of beans, nuts, seeds, and whole grains, along with chicken and meat. Whenever possible, consider organic, free-range, grass-fed, and free-farming-precedence products.

Please note that cruciferous vegetables like broccoli, Brussels sprouts, cabbage, and cauliflower are high in sulfur and may cause bloating and gas in some people. Consider taking a supplement that contains choline and methionine instead if you're experiencing abdominal distension.

- Carbs: It is recommended that you reduce the amount of carbohydrates you consume as significantly as possible to maintain liver health.

- Toxic Substances: Avoid chronic malnutrition, processed foods, margarine, canned foods, alcoholic beverages, fried food, corn syrup with a high fructose content, raw shellfish, certain medications (including acetaminophen), poisonous wild mushrooms, and being exposed to chemicals (PVC, PBA), heavy metals such as mercury, colorants, additives, and preservatives (e.g., parabens).

- Water: Drinking plenty of water during the day helps the liver operate properly and wash away toxins. Opt for at least eight glasses of water (64 ounces) per day.

Deep Hepatic Clearance

The ability of the liver to eliminate waste and toxic substances in the blood is referred to as deep hepatic clearance. The liver plays an important role in our general wellness by performing a range of processes, such as detoxification of toxic substances, drug and hormone metabolism, and bile synthesis for digestion. The hepatic artery (HA) and portal vein supply blood to the liver, which provides nutrients and oxygen to the liver cells. The liver's cells, or hepatocytes, are in charge of extracting waste and toxic substances from the blood circulation.

Deep hepatic clearance is made up of multiple complex mechanisms that take place within the liver cells. The transformation of lipophilic (fat-soluble) molecules into more water-soluble ones is a crucial process known as phase I metabolism. This conversion makes it easier for the substances to be excreted from the body. A group of enzymes known as cytochrome P450 enzymes undertakes phase I metabolism.

After phase I metabolic processes, the compounds move through phase II metabolism, which involves the addition of a polar group to the molecules. As a result, the chemicals are made more water-soluble, and therefore, simpler to defecate. Enzymes, including glutathione S-transferases, sulfotransferases, and glucuronosyltransferases, carry out phase II metabolism.

The liver performs various critical activities that assist with deep hepatic clearance while also contributing to phase I and phase II metabolism. These include the production of bile, which is required for fat digestion and absorption, as well as the absorption of fat-soluble vitamins. Bile additionally helps in the elimination of toxins and waste substances from the body. The liver additionally maintains glucose as glycogen, which it can release into the bloodstream to keep blood sugar levels stable during fasting or physical activity.

Sustaining a healthy liver is extremely important for both deep hepatic clearance and general health. Lifestyle decisions such as a good diet, frequent exercise, and abstaining from alcohol and other harmful substances can all assist with healthy liver function. Furthermore, nutrients, including antioxidant compounds, vitamin B complex, and choline, are able to promote liver function and health.

Who Can Do It? What Does Hepatic Steatosis Mean?

Before undertaking any deep hepatic clearance regimen, contact a physician to determine whether it is safe and appropriate for your specific health conditions. A simple blood test can also be performed by your physician to establish how well your liver is functioning and to advise you about the most effective course of action to enhance your liver health.

It is also important to comprehend the concept of hepatic steatosis, which refers to the formation of fat in the liver that, if left untreated, can lead to liver damage. It is frequently connected with lifestyle variables involving excessive alcohol intake, a diet rich in fat, obesity, and diabetes. Therefore, proactively addressing hepatic steatosis and promoting liver health can have a major impact on overall health and well-being.

Who Should Not Do It?

There are certain people who shouldn't attempt deep hepatic clearance without consulting with their physician. These are some examples:

- Individuals who recently underwent a transplant of organs or are going through a stressful phase should avoid liver cleaning treatments.

- Based on studies, liver damage triggered by herbs and nutritional supplements is increasing. The caffeine in green tea extract, for example, can induce hepatitis-like damage.

- Women who are pregnant or breastfeeding should avoid using milk thistle. People who have a past history of hormone-related malignancies, such as breast, uterine, or prostate cancer, should also avoid milk thistle. Milk thistle should be avoided by anybody who is hypersensitive or allergic to marigolds, yarrow, chamomile, ragweed, chrysanthemums, or daisies.

When Can It Be Done?

It is advised to undertake a deep hepatic clearance prior to bowel cleansing and following Candida and parasite eradication. This is due to the fact that both the liver and colon are inextricably intertwined, and an optimal colon is required for normal liver function. Furthermore, removing Candida and parasites reduces the total stress on the liver, enabling it to focus more on detoxification.

How Many Times a Year?

To keep your liver healthy, you should do a deep hepatic clearance at least once a year. The frequency, however, may change based on a person's lifestyle choices, including nutrition, alcohol intake, exposure to chemical substances in the environment, and medical history.

The ideal situation is that a deep hepatic clearance ought to be performed twice annually, especially if a gut cleansing is also being done at the same time. Because the liver is responsible for creating bile, which facilitates the breakdown of lipids and promotes the digestive process, it is important to highlight that liver cleansing should be performed before gut cleansing. Prior to beginning the gut cleanse, the liver is cleansed to make sure the gut is in good condition for functioning.

Additionally, since a gut cleansing can upset the equilibrium of positive and negative bacteria in the gut, it is necessary to replenish the gut flora and microbiome thereafter. For this reason, it is essential to seek the advice of a medical practitioner or a licensed nutritionist to guarantee that the gut flora is fully restored following the cleanse.

How to Prepare for It?

Mental preparation is required prior to performing a liver cleanse. To dedicate oneself to the cleansing process, one must be motivated and have a clear mindset. It is also recommended to alter your dietary patterns for the days preceding the liver-cleansing day. The following foods should be avoided: red meat, sweets, processed foods, sausages, and non-fermented dairy-based goods. It is advised to eat a diet high in vegetable broths, green leafy vegetables, nutritious grains, plant-based protein, and easily digestible white meats like fish or moderate amounts of chicken breast, along with a healthy fasting regimen and low-carbohydrate meals, eliminating alcohol and fried foods.

In addition to dietary adjustments, supplements that include alpha-lipoic acid, silymarin, glutathione, and milk thistle can also be considered to protect liver cell function and promote the cleansing process.

Although there are far more advantages than disadvantages stated, it is typical to feel fatigued and have difficulties concentrating on the initial day of the detoxification process. Meanwhile, these symptoms are only temporary and are expected to fade away soon. Furthermore, as a healthy liver is required for optimal gut function, the liver cleansing procedure should be carried out before a gut cleanse. In order to preserve gut health following a cleanse, it is essential to properly repopulate the flora and microbiome.

Deep Liver Cleanse: Option 1

The liver cleanse treatment is divided into two phases: preparation and cleansing (La Rosa, 2017).

Preparation Phase (Days 1-6):

The preparation phase seeks to soften every substance in the liver to facilitate removal within the cleansing phase.

What you will require is as follows:

- 9 kg of apples (1.5kg per day for 6 days), or malic acid supplements (6 doses over 6 days)

- 4 doses of magnesium sulfate (10g each)

- 1 grapefruit

- Virgin olive oil

- Mineral water

During the preparation period, one can ingest 1.5 kg of apples every day for six days in a row or consume malic acid supplements. Apples are a natural source of malic acid, although it can be difficult to get enough for six doses spread over six days. In addition to malic acid or apples, the preparation process requires virgin olive oil, grapefruit, mineral water, and a total of four doses of magnesium sulfate (10 grams each). Malic acid is easily ingested by mixing it with a 500-milliliter quantity of mineral-rich water and sipping it during the day in between meals.

Cleansing Phase (Days 7-8):

This phase takes place on days 7 and 8.

Day 7:

- Two doses of magnesium sulfate (10 grams each) should be consumed in the evening. It may be beneficial to drink it with a straw due to the bitter flavor, which increases the urge to urinate later.

- At 10 p.m. that night, a finger-tall of virgin olive oil and half a glass of grapefruit juice should be consumed before falling asleep on one's right side. It is advised to focus on sensing the organ during this period in order to heighten awareness and support the body's mental state.

Day 8:

- Take the final two doses of magnesium sulfate with a glass of water at 6 a.m. and 8 a.m. This may result in defecation and the removal of fecal waste of various hues and consistency, including concretions formed in the intestines as a result of the mixing of salts and other compounds sometimes mistaken for gallstones.

Deep Liver Cleanse: Option 2

This deep liver cleanse option is a 7-day detox plan that combines a healthy diet with lemon juice, apple juice, and extra virgin olive oil. The plan is broken down as follows:

Day 1:

- Consume 5 to 6 organic apples daily.

- Every three hours consume 5–6 glasses of natural, organic green apple juice.

- Eat a salad or natural soups with small meals, and avoid red meat, refined sugar, caffeine, alcohol, and highly processed foods.

- Drink the following one hour before bedtime: 2 tablespoons of extra virgin olive oil, 8 ounces of purified water or its equivalent, and 2 tablespoons of organic lemon juice.

Day 2-6:

- Continue to ingest 5 to 6 organic green apples and consume 5 to 6 glasses of fresh green apple juice throughout the day.

- Avoid foods that are highly processed, refined carbohydrates, red meat, tobacco, alcohol, and caffeine during the day, and only consume fresh salads and soups.

- Drink the following one hour prior to going to bed: 8 ounces of purified water or its equivalent, 2 tablespoons of extra virgin olive oil, and 2 tablespoons of organic lemon juice.

Day 7:

- Before you eat again in the morning, use an enema (at your convenience) to remove any lingering toxins from the colon.

- Consume 5 to 6 organic apples during the day, and every three hours, drink 5 to 6 glasses of organic green apple juice.

- Consume veggies or natural soups with small meals and steer away from red meat, processed sugary treats, alcohol, caffeine, and highly processed foods.

- Drink the following one hour before bedtime: 8 ounces of purified water or its equivalent, 2 tablespoons of extra virgin olive oil, and 2 tablespoons of fresh lemon juice.

- Adding detoxifying tea to a daytime beverage plan is optional.

Other Factors to Consider

Addressing any parasite infections and getting rid of candida are other things to think about when undertaking a liver cleansing in order to have better results. Remnants of these frequently persist in common bile ducts and resist the effects of antiparasitic medications. Physicians typically recommend an O&P test to look for parasites, and a blood culture sample test is utilized to find candida. A microbiome test examines someone's gut flora in a stool sample.

It is also vital to remember that any intestinal cleanse should come after the liver cleanse. This is due to the fact that waste is eliminated from the bile ducts and common bile ducts at the very beginning of the small intestine during the liver's cleansing process. As a result, cleaning the gut first would be futile, and waste generated throughout the liver's cleanse cycle would contaminate it.

Chapter 3

GUT CLEANSE

The human body is a complex system with so many interconnections that science is still trying to fully understand it. The relationship between the gut and the brain is among the most intriguing and significant ones to be found in recent years. Numerous key processes that are essential for a person's overall health and welfare are carried out by the gut, or more specifically, the intestines. These processes comprise the digestion of food, the discharge of waste, and the management of the immune system.

However, the gut does more than just these fundamental duties. The enteric nervous system, also referred to as the intestinal lining, is made up of an intricate network of neurons and other cells, according to recent studies. This network, which may function autonomously from the brain inside the head, is often referred to as the "second brain." The flow of nutrition throughout the intestines, the release of digestive enzymes, and the absorption of nutrients are just a few of the many processes of the gut that are regulated by the enteric nervous system.

It is particularly intriguing how the gut and the brain are related in previously unknown ways. The gut and brain are constantly communicating with one another, with the gut transmitting signals to the brain and the brain receiving them, and vice versa. This connection is facilitated by a range of molecules produced in the gut and transferred to the brain, including neurotransmitters and hormones.

The relationship between the gut and the brain has significant effects on general health and well-being. Inconsistencies in the gut microbiota, for instance, have been linked to a variety of health issues, such as inflammatory disorders, obesity, and depression. On the other hand, improving gut health through measures like a gut cleanse can benefit many facets of health, especially mental wellness.

This chapter will examine the function of the gastrointestinal tract, how it affects the brain, and the advantages of gut cleansing for long life and general wellness. We will also offer helpful advice on how to carry out a gut cleansing in a way that is safe and effective.

Microbiome, Parasites, Candida, and Other Fungi: Importance of PH Balance

Our entire health depends on the state of our gut, and the microbiome—the vast array of microbes that inhabit our intestines—plays a significant role in preserving that condition. These microbes, which comprise bacteria, viruses, fungus, and other microbes, are essential for digestion, immune system operation, and overall wellness. However, a dysbalanced microbiome can result in a variety of medical issues. For instance, parasites are microscopic organisms that can enter the body and remain there, resulting in symptoms like lethargy, diarrhea, and gastrointestinal discomfort. Additionally, the overgrowth of Candida and other fungi in the gut can result in yeast-related infections and additional medical conditions.

Maintaining a proper pH balance in the gut is also essential for gut health. The natural acidity of the gut aids in controlling harmful microorganisms. A diet heavy in acidic foods and light in alkaline foods, on the other hand, might throw off the pH balance and cause an excess of pathogenic microbes.

Fortunately, there are measures that you may consider to promote a healthy gut flora and preserve a good pH balance. A diet high in dietary fiber, whole-grain foods, and fermented foods can encourage the development of good gut flora. A balanced population of good gut bacteria can be restored with the assistance of probiotic supplements. A healthy microbiome can also be restored by using targeted treatments to treat parasitic or fungal illnesses. Additionally, preserving a balanced pH level through dietary and lifestyle modifications can help avoid imbalances and advance good gut health.

Intestinal Permeability? What Is It, and Why Should I Be Aware of It?

Intestinal permeability, commonly referred to as "leaky gut syndrome," is a disorder where the small intestine's lining becomes weakened, allowing potentially harmful substances like toxins, germs, and undigested food to pass through to the bloodstream. This could trigger an immune response and cause several health issues with the digestive tract and beyond by causing inflammation and changes in the gut flora.

Poor diet, chronic stress, and some pharmaceuticals such as antibiotics and non-steroidal anti-inflammatory drugs (NSAIDs) are a few of the primary reasons for intestinal permeability. In addition, it may be brought on by underlying medical problems such as celiac disease and Crohn's disease. It is critical to be mindful of intestinal permeability since it frequently goes unreported and misdiagnosed and can have a substantial influence on general health and well-being.

However, there are actions you can take that boost gut health and lower your risk of getting a leaky gut. A well-rounded diet full of organic foods, prebiotics, and probiotics can help build healthy gut flora as well as improve digestion. Gut health can also be improved by controlling stress through practices like meditation, physical exercises, and getting enough sleep.

What Is SIBO? How Do I Detect if This Is Happening to Me or Not? (Gas Production Test)

Small Intestinal Bacterial Overgrowth, or SIBO, is a medical condition that develops when the small intestine becomes overgrown with bacteria. Since the large intestine should contain the majority of the bacteria, the small intestine should typically have a low bacterial count. The overgrowth of bacteria may result in numerous uncomfortable symptoms, such as bloating, abdominal ache, diarrhea, and constipation. SIBO can also hinder the body's ability to absorb nutrients, which can lead to inflammation and other health problems. It is critical to properly diagnose SIBO because these symptoms may mimic those of other digestive diseases.

One method that can be utilized to detect SIBO is the gas production test. During this test, the patient consumes a lactulose solution, a sugar that is generally not absorbed in the small intestinal tract. Any bacteria that have been introduced will begin to ferment the sugar when the lactulose passes through the intestinal tract, producing gas. A breath test is then used to measure the gas. Additional testing, such as a sample of the small intestine aspirate or biopsy, may be required to confirm the diagnosis. As a result, it necessitates a complete examination by a healthcare specialist.

What Hypochlorhydria Is and How This Affects My Microbiome? (Benefits of Betaine HCL and Digestive Enzymes)

Hypochlorhydria is a medical disorder that happens when the stomach doesn't create sufficient hydrochloric acid (HCL), as is required for healthy food digestion. Insufficient hydrochloric acid causes the stomach's pH to become less acidic, which makes it easier for dangerous germs to proliferate and raises the risk of infection.

This disorder has the potential to have significant effects on the well-being of the gut microbiome. When food is not adequately digested, it may begin to ferment within the gut, causing an overgrowth of toxic bacteria and yeast. In addition to other health difficulties, including nutritional deficiencies and autoimmune diseases, this can also lead to a variety of digestive problems like bloating, gas, and diarrhea.

Fortunately, digestive enzymes and betaine HCL can be used to treat hypochlorhydria. Betaine HCL is a natural and potent digestive chemical found in beets, spinach, and other foods that can help accelerate the formation of stomach acid. If you take a betaine HCL supplement with a meal, you can monitor yourself to see if your digestion changes or if symptoms like bloating, gas, or indigestion start to emerge to see if you have hypochlorhydria. Additionally, digestive enzymes can help break down food, especially for people with pancreatic insufficiency. They can also improve overall gut health and assist in reducing hypochlorhydria-related symptoms.

The Heidelberg pH test is a simple test for measuring stomach acid levels that includes eating a capsule carrying a pH-sensitive radio transmitter that monitors stomach acidity. In general, maintaining a healthy level of stomach acid is necessary for maintaining good gut health and preventing several kinds of diseases.

Main Reasons Why We Should Perform an Intestine or Colon Cleanse

A intestine or colon cleanse is a useful procedure for enhancing general health and well-being. The following are some of the key reasons for considering an intestine/colon cleanse:

1. To eliminate toxins: Our body's intestines and colon are in charge of eliminating waste and toxins. Toxins may accumulate in the colon when it is not operating properly, causing a variety of health concerns. An intestine/colon cleanse can help drain and eliminate harmful toxins, reduce inflammation, and boost energy levels.

2. To enhance digestion: A clogged colon can cause bloating, constipation, and other digestive problems by slowing down the digestive process. This waste can be eliminated with an intestine/colon cleanse, which will improve the efficiency of your digestive system.

3. To strengthen one's immune system: The gut contains a diverse range of bacteria, a few of which are good for human health.

When the proper balance of these bacteria is disturbed, the immune system becomes compromised, making us more susceptible to disease. An intestine/colon cleansing can assist in rebalancing the gut microbiome, enhancing general immune function.

4. To aid weight loss: Once the colon gets clogged with waste, it can result in weight gain and difficulty losing weight. You can help eliminate this waste and kickstart your weight loss efforts by performing an intestine/colon cleanse.

5. To improve skin health: Our gut health is directly linked to the overall health of our skin. A colon/intestinal cleanse may be useful in enhancing gut health, which can result in clearer, healthier skin.

What Do We Need to Consider During the Cleanse?

There are various important factors to consider throughout an intestine or colon cleanse to ensure its safety and efficacy. The points that follow are important things that you ought to keep in mind:

1. Nutrition: When undertaking a cleanse, it is necessary to consume a diet high in dietary fiber, vegetables, fruits, and whole grains.

This can help relieve constipation and maintain the health of the digestive tract. Eliminate foods that are sugary and processed because they can disturb the microbiome and cause inflammation.

2. Hydration: Staying hydrated is essential throughout the cleanse, as it aids in the removal of waste products and toxins from the body. The body may stay hydrated while stimulating regular bowel movements by consuming enough water and other fluids like fresh juices and herbal teas.

3. Exercises: Regular exercise can support the body's process of removing waste by promoting bowel movements. Walking, yoga, or other gentle workouts can be extremely helpful when on a cleanse.

4. Rest: Lack of sleep and stress can impair the body's capacity to adequately cleanse and remove waste. Prioritizing rest and relaxation while on a cleanse means getting enough sleep, lowering your stress level, and using relaxation techniques like deep breathing or meditation.

5. Supplements: Many supplements, like digestive enzymes, probiotics, and herbal medicines such as aloe vera and slippery elm,

can be beneficial during a cleanse. Probiotics can help restore healthy gut flora, and digestive enzymes can help with nutritional breakdown and absorption. Using herbs can increase waste removal and control bowel movements.

6. Consult with a medical expert: It is advised to consult with a medical expert, such as a healthcare practitioner or a nutritionist, to make sure the cleanse is secure and suitable for your particular requirements. They can also offer advice on diet, vitamins, and other lifestyle choices that will benefit and support the cleanse and general gut health.

Who Shouldn't Perform a Colon Cleanse?

While many people can benefit from an intestine/colon cleanse, certain people should steer clear of it or consult with their physician before conducting one. These include:

1. Individuals who use specific medications

2. Elderly people

3. Pregnant or breastfeeding women

4. Individuals who have a history of bowel obstruction or have had surgery

5. Individuals who have specific medical conditions

6. Individuals who have intestinal fistulas should avoid colon cleansing because it may worsen their condition.

How to Keep Your Intestine Happy and Healthy?

To keep your intestines healthy, eat a well-balanced, filled with nutrients diet rich in fiber-rich vegetables, fruit, and whole grains. Sufficient water is also necessary for the digestive system to function properly. Exercise on a regular basis can help increase intestinal motility and lower the likelihood of constipation. Stress management through relaxation practices such as deep breathing, meditation, and yoga can help improve gut health. Avoiding cigarettes and drinking excessively, as well as limiting the consumption of refined and high-fat meals, can help lower your chance of developing inflammation of the gut and other digestive diseases. Finally, including prebiotics and probiotics in your diet can aid in the development of beneficial gut microbes and the maintenance of a healthy microbiome.

The Most Common Signs of an Unhealthy Intestine

To address any problems as soon as they arise, it's crucial to be mindful of the most prevalent symptoms of an unhealthy intestine. Chronic diarrhea or constipation, which might suggest a disturbance in the gut flora or an absence of fiber in the diet, constitutes one of the most visible symptoms. Severe gas and bloating are other typical symptoms, which might be caused by a bacterial overgrowth or an allergy to specific foods.

Other symptoms of an infected intestine include pain in the abdomen, discomfort, and pain, which can be brought on by infection, inflammation, or a condition called irritable bowel syndrome. Acne, rashes, and eczema can be additionally connected to an unhealthy gut, as skin conditions are typically a reflection of what's going on inside the body. In addition, lower immunity, recurring infections, and intolerance can all be signs of a faulty gut.

Lastly, psychological disorders such as sadness and anxiety may be linked to an abnormal gut. The digestive system and brain are inextricably linked, and a poor digestive system may result in an imbalance in neurotransmitter production, which affects mood and cognitive performance. It is critical to address any indicators of a problematic gut as soon as possible because they might have an influence on general health and well-being.

Daily Tip to Keep Our Intestine Healthy

Making small attempts every day can make a big difference in maintaining a healthy gut. Here's a daily tip to help your intestines stay healthy:

Include Fiber-Rich Meals in Your Diet:

Make an effort to include a range of fiber-rich foods in your regular diet. Fiber is essential for intestine health because it facilitates digestion, regulates bowel motions, and promotes the formation of good bacteria in the gut. Consume a variety of soluble and insoluble fibers from nuts, vegetables, whole grains, fruits, legumes, and olives.

Begin the day with a fiber-rich breakfast of oats served with berries and a sprinkle of chia seeds. Lunch ought to include a colorful bowl with leafy greens, veggies, and legumes, and dinner should include full-grain alternatives like brown rice or quinoa. To increase your fiber intake, nibble on juicy fruits or vegetable slices throughout the day.

Remember to gradually increase the amount of fiber you consume in order for your body to acclimate and avoid intestinal pain. Drink ample amounts of pure water throughout the day to stay hydrated, as fiber performs best when accompanied by proper fluid intake.

By integrating fiber-rich foods throughout your everyday meals, you can encourage regular bowel movements, an optimal digestive environment, and overall intestinal health.

When and How Often Is It Recommended to Do a Colon Cleanse?

The duration and frequency of colon cleansing can vary depending on personal circumstances and preferences. Before beginning any cleanse, it is critical to exercise caution and check with a healthcare practitioner. These are some general ideas:

1. Periodic Cleansing: People with a digestive system that is functioning properly may perform periodic colon cleansing as a type of detoxification or to maintain regular bowel movements. This should be performed either once or every two years or more frequently if indicated by a healthcare practitioner.

2. Medical Concerns: Whether you're experiencing specific digestive disorders or health conditions, you should check with your physician to establish if a colon cleansing is appropriate for you and how of-

ten you should perform it. Certain medical disorders, such as irritable bowel syndrome, diverticulitis, or major/recent abdominal surgery, may necessitate caution or abstinence from colon cleansing.

3. Listen to Your Own Body: It is of the utmost importance that you pay attention to your body's messages and respond appropriately. If you are suffering symptoms such as bloating, irritable bowel syndrome, or digestive discomfort, a colon cleansing may be necessary. Nevertheless, constantly seek the advice of a medical professional to discover the root cause and the best course of action.

4. Lifestyle Choices and Diet: The necessity for colon cleansing is also influenced by your daily habits and dietary choices. If you eat a diet packed with refined foods that are lacking in fiber or if you indulge in harmful lifestyle choices like smoking or drinking excessively, you might want to consider colon cleansing on a regular basis to promote overall gut health.

In-Depth Small Intestine Cleanse: Shank Prakshalana Method

The Shank Prakshalana technique is a traditional yogic purification that involves the small intestine. It is a potent treatment for removing waste products and toxins from the intestines and for increasing general wellness and vitality. Below is an in-depth look into the Shank Prakshalana approach to cleansing the small intestine:

1. Preparation: It is vital that you prepare your body prior to commencing the cleanse. Begin by eating a light diet of fruits, veggies, and whole grains in the days preceding the cleansing. This will smooth the transfer as well as render the process more efficient.

2. Duration: The Shank Prakshalana procedure typically occurs on an empty stomach in the morning. Because the treatment requires frequent excretion, it is best to do it on a day when you've got plenty of time and can be near a restroom.

3. Saltwater Solution: To begin the cleanse, make a saline solution by simply dissolving two tablespoons of natural salt in a liter of warm water. To avoid any negative effects, it is important to use non-iodized salt. The saltwater solution creates a slight osmotic

effect, which draws water towards the intestinal tract and accelerates the cleansing process.

4. Practice sequence: Place yourself in a relaxed position with a towel close by. Drink between two and three glasses of the saltwater solution before beginning a sequence of specific yoga asanas, postures, and exercises. The sequence often consists of poses such as Kati Chakrasana (Standing Spinal Twist), Tiryaka Tadasana (Swaying Palm Tree Pose), and Tadasana (Mountain Pose). These movements contribute to the stimulation of peristalsis and the removal of waste products from the small intestinal tract.

5. Flushing Procedure: After finishing the first round of exercises, keep on drinking the saltwater solution and rotating through the asanas. This practice is repeated repeatedly until the water is expelled from the body system, indicating that the small intestine has been thoroughly cleansed.

6. Rehydration: After the process of elimination is over, it is important to take a rest to enable the body to recuperate. To rehydrate and top off on fluids, consume a lot of warm water or herbal tea. Avoid eating anything solid for a few hours to allow your digestive

system to relax.

The Shank Prakshalana method is a rigorous practice that should be studied by an experienced yoga instructor or practitioner who can properly assist you through the process. It is recommended to have it done two to four times a year, depending on an individual's health and digestive function; however, it is not for everyone and may not be suited for people with certain health concerns or during pregnancy. Before beginning any intensive cleansing technique, always discuss it with a healthcare expert. Remember that a small intestine cleansing, such as Shank Prakshalana, should be done with caution and sensitivity to your body's boundaries. It's crucial to pay attention to your body's cues and stop the procedure if you feel extreme discomfort or unfavorable effects.

Coffee Enema

Coffee enemas have acquired favor as a liver cleansing treatment as well as an enema owing to their possible detoxification advantages. The caffeine in the coffee is taken into the bloodstream and travels to the liver during this process, where it is transformed into a strong detoxifier. This stimulation causes the liver to create more bile, which assists in the clearance of toxins by guiding them to the small intestine. This procedure facilitates the removal of toxins that accumulate within organs, tissues, and the bloodstream. Coffee includes alkaloids, which help the liver detoxify by promoting the synthesis of particular enzymes. Coffee enemas can help with toxin clearance by stimulating bile secretion and enhancing liver function. To summarize, a coffee enema speeds up the process of detoxification and reduces toxic substance buildup in the gut. To guarantee safety and effectiveness, coffee enemas should be administered carefully and under adequate supervision.

In-Depth Colon Cleanse

Enemas have grown in popularity as a method of colon cleansing and detoxification. They can be given by a specialist using a method called "Colon Hydrotherapy," which is strongly advised, or they can be administered at home using an enema kit containing natural and organic fluids like saline or coffee mixtures.

When administering an enema at home, suspend the kit from one to one and a half meters above the body. The fluid must be kept at an even temperature in the sigmoid colon (the final portion of the colon) for around 30 minutes. This mechanism causes sigmoid colon distension, which increases peristalsis not solely in the area of the sigmoid colon but additionally in the intestinal tract, leading to an intense feeling of evacuation.

You can successfully evacuate feces and experience a forceful contraction of all areas of the intestines by utilizing this procedure. This aids in the removal of sluggish proteins that have not been properly digested, as well as old fecal waste stuck to the intestinal mucosa walls. It is crucial to remove these residues since they can function as cancer precursors. It's worth noting that doing an enema treatment at home can be more painful than going through colonic hydrotherapy with a specialized flow system.

Importance of Recovering the Microbiome

There are three basic methods for repopulating and improving your gut microbiome, each of which plays an important role in regaining and sustaining your gut health.

1. The first method is microbiome intake, which attempts to ensure the consumption of a diverse variety of beneficial strains as quickly as possible following an intestinal cleaning. This can be accomplished through the consumption of probiotics, which is thought to be the most effective and effi-

cient approach. Probiotics are specially designed to give an excessive amount of helpful bacteria straight to the gut, thereby assisting in the restoration of microbiota balance. You can additionally boost your consumption of fermented products, although this approach might go slower and provide a more limited choice of strains. Microbes generate fermented foods such as kefir, yogurt, cheese, sauerkraut, kombucha, and kimchi, which contain a variety of healthful bacterial species such as Lactobacilli. These foods can help restore a healthy gut microbiota, especially after antibiotic treatment. It's important to take into account a few things while introducing fermented foods into your diet. To begin, make sure you are not allergic to fermented foods because some people may have negative reactions. Furthermore, it is critical to choose fermented foods that have not been pasteurized, as this process might destroy beneficial bacteria. Organic fermented foods are also recommended because herbicides such as glyphosate might disrupt the ground microorganisms and consequently damage the gut microbiota. Finally, be mindful that each fermented item contains only a few strains; ensuring a variety of different fermented food items will guarantee a wide diversity of strains, avoiding the overgrowth of only a few

2. The second method to improve your intestinal microbiome is to feed the healthy bacteria that live in your gut. This strategy focuses on supplying the nutrients required for favorable strains to develop. Feeding healthy bacteria starts with consuming soluble fiber on a daily basis. Soluble fibers, such as xylooligosaccharides, are found in a variety of foods, such as honey and vegetables. These fibers work as prebiotics, providing nutrition to the good bacteria in your gut. Consuming foods high in fructooligosaccharides, like garlic, artichoke, leek, asparagus, and berries, provides additional fuel for the beneficial bacteria, encouraging their growth and activity. Consumption of substances such as soluble fibers and fructooligosaccharides contributes to the growth of beneficial bacteria. They act as a source of energy for these bacteria, allowing them to create necessary molecules, such as short-chain fatty acids, that provide several health benefits. Furthermore, these fibers are fermented by the gut bacteria, which results in the creation of metabolites that support the overall health and functionality of the gut.

3. The third main method for repopulating and enhancing your intestinal microbiome is fecal microbiota transplantation (FMT). This method involves transferring feces from a donor who is in good health to the recipient's gastrointestinal tract, delivering a varied range of helpful bacteria. FMT has the potential to be an effective method for recovering microbial balance and fostering an optimal gut environment. When planning FMT, it is advisable to begin by preparing the gut by consuming probiotics containing a diverse range of strains, preferably more than 30 strains. These probiotics prepare the digestive tract for transplantation. Following that, it has to be essential to consume a large amount of soluble fiber to promote the development of the introduced bacteria. This helps to generate an environment conducive to the development and expansion of the transplant microbiota. Specific probiotic strains can further improve gut health in addition to soluble fiber and probiotics. Among the prominent strains are:

- Bifidobacterium Bifidum: It is well-known for its capacity to boost neurotransmitter production, like serotonin and GABA, which help with mood management, relaxation, and sleep quality.

- Saccharomyces cerevisiae: Stimulates the synthesis of noradrenaline, a neurotransmitter linked to enhanced energy levels.

- Bacillus family: Increases the production of dopamine, a pleasure hormone that can improve mood and well-being.

- Lactobacillus casei and paracasei: These strains support lactase synthesis, which makes lactose digestion easier and helps to treat irritable bowel syndrome.

- Lactobacillus Acidophilus: Supports lactase creation, which is especially helpful for people who experience reduced lactose tolerance due to age.

- Lactobacillus plantarum: It assists in improving intestinal permeability and could potentially be useful in treating allergies.

- Lactobacillus rhamnosus GR-1 and L. fermentum RC: These strains have been researched for their potential benefits in treating vaginal candidiasis and urinary tract infections.

Researchers are increasingly focused on microbiome supplementation, which includes the use of probiotics to promote the growth of beneficial bacteria. Furthermore, research into prebiotics, which are compounds that serve as food for bacteria, is starting to gain traction as an innovative method for feeding the microbiome. Another area of study is modbiotics, which are substances that help control the balance and interactions of bacteria in the microbiome. Furthermore, the synthesis of postbiotics, which are metabolic byproducts of helpful bacteria, has received a lot of attention and praise. New editions of this book are anticipated to address these new subjects, which reflect the achievements and changing knowledge in the area of microbiome research.

Why and How to Do It ASAP?

Restoring and recovering an optimal microbiome is vital for your general well-being, and acting quickly can considerably help your health. Here is why and how you should prioritize your microbiome recovery as soon as possible:

1. Optimizing Treatment Efficacy: If you're taking medical treatments that can upset your microbiome, such as chemotherapy, antibiotics, or other interventions, it's important to take urgent action to recover and restore balance. By acting quickly, you can enhance the efficacy of these medicines by bolstering your body's inherent defenses and improving treatment outcomes.

2. Reducing Discomfort and Symptoms: Microbiome imbalances can produce a variety of unpleasant symptoms that involve gas, abdominal pain, bloating, diarrhea, and constipation. Restoring the microbiome as soon as possible will help relieve these symptoms while also improving your overall ease and quality of life.

3. Avoiding Potential Imbalances: Having an imbalanced microbiome can cause a variety of health problems, including digestive disorders, reduced immune responses, inflammatory disorders, and mental health issues. By resolving this imbalance as soon as possible, you can keep these issues from deteriorating and reduce your chances of having more serious illnesses in the long run.

So, how could you prioritize your microbiome recovery as promptly as possible? Here are some essential measures to take:

- Avoiding Harmful Substances: Reduce your consumption of processed meals, refined sugars, artificial flavors, and other things that can upset the microbiota. Reduce the use of unneeded drugs, particularly antibiotics, unless your physician has recommended them.

- Taking Probiotic Supplements: Probiotics might help in the introduction of good microorganisms into your gut. Pick a high-quality supplement with a range of strains and take it as directed. Consult with your physician to identify the best probiotic for what you need specifically.

- Maintain a Balanced Diet: Aim for a diet that promotes a varied and balanced microbiota. Include fiber-rich foods like vegetables, fruits, grains, and nuts in your diet since they supply important nutrients for the formation of healthy bacteria.

- Stay Hydrated: Consuming plenty of water supports good digestion and helps in the maintenance of a balanced microbiota. Drink plenty of water during the day to promote good gut health.

- Minimize Stress: Chronic stress has been shown to have a deleterious impact on the microbiota. To promote a healthy microbiome, use stress-reduction tactics such as physical activity, breathing exercises, meditation, and engaging in activities you enjoy.

Keep in mind that the restoration and recovery of a healthy microbiome is a slow and steady process that demands perseverance and patience. You can

improve your general health and microbiota by taking quick action and applying these measures.

Chapter 4

Respiratory Tract Cleanse

The human body is an incredible masterpiece of intricate structures that operate in unison to support life. Among these intricate structures, the respiratory tract plays a vital role in preserving our lives and well-being. The respiratory system acts as a portal for oxygen to flow into our bodies and for carbon dioxide to be released, beginning with our first breath and continuing through the countless number of breaths that we take throughout our lives. However, just like any other organ of our body, it may build up pollutants, toxins, and other harmful substances over time, affecting its function and threatening our health.

This chapter looks at respiratory tract cleansing as a valuable technique for reviving and rejuvenating this crucial system. We will look at many methods and strategies for properly cleansing the respiratory tract, removing accumulated pollutants, and restoring its ideal function. Through targeted cleansing methods, we are able to eliminate harmful substances such as pollutants, allergies, and irritants that frequently enter our respiratory system. By doing so, we create an atmosphere that fosters overall respiratory wellness while supporting optimal lung health and oxygenation.

During our exploration of cleansing strategies, we provide a variety of natural ways that can be simply implemented into our everyday practice. We discuss the advantages of all-natural lung cleansing activities, including breathing techniques, steam inhaling, and saline treatments, in tackling mucus and respiratory disorders such as COPD (chronic obstructive pulmonary disease), bronchitis, asthma, sinus problems, and coughing. So take a deep breath and start on this illuminating journey through the respiratory system. Discover the keys to a cleansed and rejuvenated respiratory system, and you'll be on the path to optimal health and longevity.

How the Respiratory Tract Deals With Toxins

The respiratory tract has exceptional capabilities for dealing with toxins in the environment that we breathe. Our respiratory system launches a number of defense measures for the protection of our lungs and preserves its full functionality the moment air penetrates our nose. The nasal passageways serve as the very first line of defense. Small hairs inside the nostrils, known as "cilia," serve as filters, capturing bigger dust and pollution-related particles. Additionally, nasal mucus helps trap and immobilize tiny particles such as germs, viruses, and toxic substances.

As air moves deeper into the respiratory tract, it eventually gets to the bronchial tubes and the lungs. The airways in the bronchi are coated with cilia, which pulse in rhythmic waves to move nasal mucus and stuck particles upward into the throat. The elimination of toxins and other foreign compounds from the airways is facilitated by a process termed mucociliary clearance. Toxins are dealt with in the lungs by specialized cells known as macrophages. Macrophages are immune system cells that operate as scavengers, absorbing and neutralizing hazardous particles and germs via a process known as phagocytosis. This system facilitates the elimination of toxins and infections, keeping them from harming the lungs.

Furthermore, the respiratory tract contains built-in defense mechanisms for dealing with harmful substances. The cough reflex is triggered when the lungs come into contact with irritants or toxic substances. Coughing releases toxic substances, mucus, and other foreign particles from the respiratory tract. Sneezing functions in a similar way, removing allergens and pollutants from the nasal passages. Whenever the respiratory tract is exposed to toxins, inflammatory responses are activated. Toxins are isolated and contained by inflammation, preventing them from spreading deeper into the lungs. However, long-term inflammation brought on by toxin exposure can harm lung tissue and exacerbate respiratory disorders.

The multifaceted interaction of physical barriers, generation of mucus, ciliary movement, immunological reactions, coughing reflexes, and inflammation enables the respiratory system to cope effectively with toxins and pollutants. These defenses act in tandem to prevent dangerous substances from entering the fragile lung tissues while helping maintain a healthy respiratory system. However, it is important to recognize that continuous or extensive exposure to toxins may compromise the respiratory tract's built-in defenses. Smoking, hazardous jobs, poor air quality, and other factors can interfere with the efficiency of these defenses, resulting in respiratory problems and an increased risk of infection. Understanding how our lungs and respiratory system respond to toxins gives us the ability to take proactive steps to protect our wellness and promote optimal lung function.

Ways to Cleanse Your Respiratory Tract

The respiratory tract is essential to our general health because it filters and manages toxins that enter our bodies through many different pathways. Toxic substances enter our bodies mostly through the digestive and respiratory systems, with only a minor fraction entering through the skin.

Within the respiratory system, saline solution can be used at home to perform a nostril saline solution rinse, commonly referred to as nasal irrigation or nasal douching, as well as sinus massage techniques that can help reduce congestion. A lesser-known cleansing treatment known as Proetz can be quite effective for people suffering from allergies, sinus mucus buildup, chronic rhinitis, and sinusitis. A saline solution is used in the Proetz procedure to successfully clear the sinuses by being forced into one of the nostrils and retrieved from the other. This simple treatment, frequently administered by otorhinolaryngologists, allows for repeated sinus cleansing, minimizing inflammation, chronic sinusitis, and the influence of allergies on the airways. It has a cleansing function that helps eliminate pollutants from the respiratory tract without any harmful or adverse effects.

However, it is important to emphasize that there isn't currently a system in place that could effectively detoxify the lungs at the respiratory level. The primary focus is mainly on cleansing methods or treatments that assist in toxin removal from the sinuses and upper airways. Deep breathing practices, steam inhalation, saline nasal irrigation, staying adequately hydrated, and herbal remedies are a few other respiratory cleansing techniques that we can use to help the body's natural cleansing processes, lessen the load of toxins, and maintain optimum lung health.

Tips to Avoid Exposure to Air Pollutants That Can Damage Your Lungs

To keep your respiratory tract healthy, you should limit the amount of time you are exposed to air pollutants, sources of moisture, and mold, as well as other potential irritants that may harm your lungs. Here are some tips you might consider to avoid exposure and maintain your respiratory health:

1. Maintain a clean indoor air quality environment by closing windows during times of high outdoor pollution, utilizing air purifiers, and removing indoor pollutants like dust and pet dander.

2. Proactively detect and treat any occurrences of moisture and address any indicators of mold formation within your living space as soon as possible.

3. Wear protective masks when exposed to harmful airborne pollutants that consist of dust, chemicals, or smoke.

4. If you must apply herbicides or pesticides within or surrounding your house, carefully follow the instructions on the label and utilize them in a way that limits your and others' exposure.

5. To prevent respiratory harm, avoid smoking and exposure to secondhand smoke.

6. Be aware that indoor pollutants such as chemical cleaning products, volatile organic compounds (VOCs), and some construction materials such as paints can all have a negative impact on your respiratory health.

7. When possible, avoid industrial and high-traffic areas.

8. Keep up-to-date on the air quality in your neighborhood and change your activities accordingly.

9. Avoid being outside when pollution levels are at their highest and opt for periods when the air quality is at its best.

Why Is It So Important to Keep Your Respiratory Tract Healthy?

Sustaining an optimal respiratory tract is important for a number of reasons, including:

1. Disease Prevention: By maintaining a healthy respiratory tract, you can minimize your risk of developing respiratory disorders such as chronic obstructive pulmonary disease (COPD), asthma, pneumonia, and bronchitis.

2. Respiratory Function: A functional respiratory tract allows for efficient breathing and an appropriate flow of gases, permitting the respiratory system to function efficiently.

3. Life Quality: Having good respiratory health improves your capacity to breathe easily, sleep well, and participate in everyday activities, which improves the general quality of life.

4. Oxygen Supply: The respiratory system supplies a consistent supply of life-sustaining oxygen to the human body's cells, supporting important processes and overall well-being.

5. Immuno Defense: It protects you from respiratory infections and diseases by act-

ing as a primary defense against airborne pathogens, allergens, and toxins.

Simple Methods and Therapies That Can Be Added to Our Daily Routine to Cleanse Our Respiratory Tract

Simple methods and therapies may contribute to a significant difference in the purification and ongoing upkeep of your respiratory system's health. Here are some beneficial routines to include in your everyday routine:

- Herbal teas with relaxing elements such as peppermint, fresh ginger, or chamomile can help alleviate respiratory congestion.

- Maintaining good posture and including chest expansion techniques to assist with opening up the chest cavity, enhance lung capacity, and allow for deeper breathing.

- To enhance relaxation, reduce tension, and maximize respiratory function, try different breathing techniques such as diaphragmatic respiration or alternate nostril breathing.

- Make sure your workspace and living areas are adequately ventilated to minimize pollutants in the indoor environment and enhance air quality. Open windows or use fans to improve air circulation. Look into using air dehumidifiers or purifiers to improve indoor air quality.

- Maintain a clean environment free of dirt, pet hair, and any other allergens that might cause respiratory issues. Maintain a healthy interior atmosphere by vacuuming, dusting, and washing bedding on a regular basis. Moreover, adequate ventilation and the use of air purifiers or dehumidifiers can also help improve indoor air quality and efficiently address damp and mold issues.

- Get sufficient restful sleep and create a comfortable sleeping environment. Sleep promotes immunological function as well as general respiratory health.

Natural Ways to Cleanse Your Lungs

There are a variety of ways and lifestyle changes that can help with clearer lungs and easier breathing. These basic practices can be easily incorporated into your everyday routine, providing you with a route towards a healthier respiratory system:

1. Using Steam: Steam treatment, also known as steam inhalation, functions as a relaxing balm for your airways. Inhaling water vapor can help open up the airways and loosen

sticky mucus. Steam's warmth and moisture produce an atmosphere that promotes improved breathing as well as efficient mucus clearance. Although steam treatment has shown encouraging results in delivering instant relief, more scientific research is needed to fully understand its potential for improving lung health.

2. The Technique of Regulated Coughing: Coughing is the body's natural method for expelling toxins trapped in mucus. Individuals can remove extra mucus from their airways by completing a sequence of actions with controlled coughing. To efficiently remove mucus and cleanse the airways, maintain an upright seated position, inhale through the nose, lean forward while exhaling and coughing, and maintain a slightly open mouth.

3. Improving Postural Drainage: The process of postural drainage uses gravity to remove mucus from the lungs. You can help facilitate the normal passage of mucus out of your airways by resting on your back, side, or stomach. The effectiveness of this practice is increased by combining these positions with appropriate breathing methods, which also help with breathing and reduce the risk of

developing lung infections.

4. Green Tea's Healing Power: Because of its high antioxidant content, green tea may hold the key to lowering lung inflammation. It has been discovered that these antioxidants can preserve lung tissue and lessen the harmful effects of smoke inhalation. A Korean study revealed that people who drank no less than two to three cups of green tea per day had better lung health than those who did not.

5. Embracing Anti-Inflammatory Foods: Reducing inflammation in the airways will help you breathe easier and take a load off your chest. Incorporating anti-inflammatory items into your diet can help you fight inflammation. Turmeric, green leafy vegetables, blueberries, walnuts, and beans are just a few of the foods with anti-inflammatory characteristics that will help your respiratory health.

6. Chest Percussion Rhythm: Chest percussion is a technique used by physicians or respiratory therapists to release blocked mucus from the lungs. When paired with postural drainage, this approach aids in the effective removal of accumulated mucus from the airways.

7. Advantages of Exercise: Being active regularly not only improves your entire physical and emotional well-being, but it also helps your lungs stay healthy. Physical activity works your muscles, raising the pace of breathing and improving the delivery of vital oxygen to these critical organs. Exercise also improves circulation, allowing your body to easily remove carbon dioxide, a consequence of effort. Even people with chronic lung diseases can benefit from regular exercise, but it is best to discuss it with a medical professional first.

Benefits of Breathing Steam

Breathing in moist and warm steam has been shown to help relieve symptoms of infections of the upper respiratory tract and nasal congestion. The following are the primary benefits of steam inhalation:

1. Steam inhalation relieves nose discomfort and inflammation by relaxing blood vessels. This can temporarily relieve symptoms such as a stuffed-up nose, a sore throat, and dry passageways.

2. Steam's wetness can help thin out the mucus inside the sinuses, making drainage easier. By allowing the sinuses to clear more efficiently, this can help relieve congestion and

improve breathing.

3. Nasal allergies, the common cold, the flu, sinusitis, bronchitis, and other related symptoms, including headaches and coughing, may all be temporarily relieved by steam inhalation. It can help relieve pain and improve breathing.

Although inhaling steam cannot cure or eliminate viruses, it can provide subjective alleviation and promote the body's own internal healing mechanisms.

Follow these steps to practice steam inhalation:

- Bring the water to a boil, then slowly pour it into a big bowl.

- Make a tent-like enclosure with an absorbent towel over your head.

- To avoid coming into contact with steam, keep your face between eight and twelve inches from the water and your eyes closed.

- For a minimum of two to five minutes, inhale gently and deeply through your nostrils.

- Limit your sessions to ten to fifteen minutes in length and repeat as needed up to three times a day.

You can also utilize a powered steam inhaler or vaporizer, which gives a regulated discharge of steam. Keep in mind that you must wash the equipment on a regular basis in order to avoid microbiological or fungal growth.

Using Eucalyptus in Your Shower for Incredible Healing Benefits

Did you know that a simple addition to your daily shower routine can unlock the remarkable healing properties of eucalyptus? Incorporating eucalyptus leaves or essential oils into your shower environment can offer a range of aromatherapeutic advantages. Eucalyptus is an evergreen plant native to Australia that is now grown around the world. Follow these steps to experience the rejuvenating effects:

1. Get some fresh eucalyptus leaves or high-quality eucalyptus essential oil, and make sure your shower room is well-ventilated.

2. For fresh leaves, bundle a few twigs and tie them tightly. For essential oil, put a few drops on a washcloth or your diffuser.

3. Hang the eucalyptus bundle or place the oil-treated cloth in a place where it won't get wet but is within reach of the shower steam.

4. While you shower, the steam interacts with the eucalyptus, releasing its energizing aroma and healing benefits.

Benefits You May Experience:

- Eucalyptus is believed to relieve nasal congestion and improve breathing, making it an excellent choice for allergies, coughs, asthma, or sinus infections.

- While showering, the soothing scent of eucalyptus can have a calming effect on the mind, relieve stress, and promote relaxation.

- The natural antibacterial qualities of eucalyptus can help purify the air. Studies also show it may kill some viruses and fungi, which can potentially help your body's defense.

- Inhaling the invigorating scent of eucalyptus can lift your mood and give you energy for the day ahead.

Benefits of a Saline Solution to Deal With Mucus if You Have COPD, Asthma, Bronchitis, Sinus, Coughing, or Pneumonia

Saline solution, a salt-water solution, has various advantages for people suffering from chronic pulmonary disease (COPD), bronchitis, asthma, sinus issues, coughing, and pneumonia. Following are the specific reasons why the saline solution is beneficial in treating mucus-related signs and symptoms:

1. The use of saline solution is a safe, non-medicated choice for treating symptoms brought on by excess mucus. It contains no medications or chemicals and is therefore acceptable for everyday use.

2. The saline solution has a calming impact on the tissues of the respiratory system, reducing inflammation and irritation throughout the airways. Individuals suffering from illnesses such as asthma and chronic obstructive pulmonary disease (COPD), where inflammation serves as a prevalent symptom, may benefit from this.

3. The saline solution is suitable for people of all ages, including newborns, children, adults, and elderly people. It is commonly used to treat mucus-related complaints in people of all ages in a safe yet efficient manner.

4. There are many ways to use saline solution, including nasal rinses, nasal sprays, gargles, and nebulizer solutions. Individuals can choose the best strategy for them based

on their personal respiratory problems and preferences.

5. Dry airways can exacerbate respiratory symptoms and cause an increase in mucus production. Saline solution is a natural moisturizer that hydrates the airways and prevents dryness, inflammation, and discomfort. The saline solution promotes proper lung function by maintaining moisture in the respiratory airways.

The Amazing Ways Vitamin D Boosts Respiratory Health and Reduces Corticosteroid Resistance

Here are some of the respiratory benefits of vitamin D, including its function in polymorphism and its capacity to help reduce corticosteroid resistance:

- Respiratory System Health: Vitamin D is essential for respiratory tract health. It possesses anti-inflammatory qualities that aid in the reduction of inflammation within the airways, supporting better function of the lungs and respiratory health.

- Polymorphism: Polymorphism is the term for genetic variances among a population that might influence a person's response to specific variables, for instance, medications or foods. Vitamin D polymorphisms may influence how vitamin D is metabolized and utilized by the body. Identifying these genetic variations can help us better understand individual vitamin D demands and the implications for our lung wellness.

- Decreased Corticosteroid Resistance: These medications are routinely used to treat respiratory disorders like chronic obstructive pulmonary disease (COPD) and asthma. Due to the emergence of tolerance with repeated use, people may start to respond less favorably to the impacts of corticosteroids. Vitamin D has been proven to boost corticosteroid anti-inflammatory effects and decrease corticosteroid resistance, resulting in better treatment outcomes for people with respiratory diseases.

Benefits of Breathing Exercises

1. Box breathing: This method aims to balance out the lengths of each breath rhythm. It entails breathing, holding your breath, breathing out, and then holding your breath again for the same count. It encourages relaxation and the elimination of tension.

2. The Wim Hof Method: This technique, also known as The Iceman, combines deep

breathing, cold therapy or ice baths, and meditation to provide benefits that help increase lung capacity, improve oxygenation, enhance immune function, provide higher energy levels, reduce stress, and improve mental focus.

3. Alternate Nostril Breathing: In this technique, one nostril is alternately blocked while the other is used to inhale, and then the other nostril is used to exhale. It promotes relaxation and mental tranquility by balancing breath and energy flow.

4. Diaphragmatic Breathing: This breathing technique entails deep breathing through the expansion of the abdomen on inhalation and contracting it on exhalation. It promotes relaxation and increases lung capacity.

5. Pursed-lip Breathing: This is a technique in which you inhale gently through your nose and exhale through your pursed lips. It aids in the regulation of breathing and the maintenance of airway pressure, and it can also be helpful to people suffering from COPD or asthma.

6. 4-7-8 Breathing: This technique stresses long exhalations by breathing for four counts, holding the breath for seven counts,

and then exhaling for eight counts. It triggers the relaxation response in the body, soothes the mind, and decreases anxiety.

These breathing techniques can be implemented into your daily practice in order to enhance respiratory function, control stress, and promote overall well-being. Begin with moderate, gentle practice and gradually increase the intensity as you feel comfortable.

Benefits of Breathing Well While Sleeping: Buteyko Method Breathing Exercises

Breathing properly while sleeping, particularly with the use of Buteyko Method breathing techniques, has a number of advantages. Here are a few examples:

- Improved Respiratory Health: Because the Buteyko Method concentrates on airflow through the nose and reduces overbreathing, it can help strengthen respiratory muscles and enhance lung function. This is particularly beneficial for people who have respiratory disorders, including bronchitis, asthma, and chronic obstructive pulmonary disease (COPD).

- Reduced Snoring and Sleeping Apnea: The Buteyko technique places an emphasis on breathing through the nose and maintaining ideal carbon dioxide levels. This can help minimize snoring and indicators of sleep apnea, which is a disorder marked by pauses in airflow while sleeping.

- Increased Energy and Vitality: The Buteyko Method optimizes respiratory function and increases oxygen intake through enhanced breathing practices. This can lead to more energy, better physical performance, and an increased sensation of vitality throughout the course of the day.

- Improved Concentration and Mental Clarity: Proper breathing while sleeping can increase oxygenation to the brain, which improves cognitive function, focus, and mental clarity when you wake up. This can help with general cognitive performance and productivity throughout the course of your day.

- Reduce Nighttime Difficulties: People with respiratory diseases frequently have symptoms that occur at night, such as wheezing, coughing, or shortness of breath. Using the Buteyko approach before going to bed will help ease these symptoms and allow for a more tranquil and undisturbed night's sleep.

Alternative Methods

Alternative methods, in addition to traditional medical treatments, provide patients with alternate options for supporting their respiratory health. These methods include a variety of herbal therapies and techniques aimed at improving lung function, alleviating symptoms, and promoting overall well-being. While each treatment has its own distinct qualities, they all share the common goal of giving people more alternatives for improving their respiratory health.

Many alternative ways promote relaxation, less stress, and improved quality of sleep, as these elements are important for respiratory health. The practice of meditation, Pranayama breathing, Yogic breathing, holotropic breathing, rebirthing breathing, transient hypofrontality breathworks, deep breathing techniques, and relaxation therapy can support the enhancement of breathing patterns, alleviate anxiety, and improve overall respiratory health.

Furthermore, specific alternative treatments such as melatonin supplementation and its relationship to the respiratory system, the advantages of continuous positive airway pressure (CPAP) treatment, ozone therapy, and infrared therapy with infrared sauna perks for lung function will be explored in depth later. These strategies provide new approaches to respiratory wellness management and have drawn attention to their possible benefits in enhancing lung function and symptom alleviation.

While alternate methods can provide additional channels for respiratory support, they shouldn't necessarily be used in place of standard medical care. Individuals can improve their overall respiratory health and quality of life by combining alternate methods with established medical approaches.

Melatonin Supplementation and Relation With the Respiratory Tract

Melatonin supplementation is gaining popularity due to its potential benefits for respiratory tract health. In addition to being a hormone, melatonin is also an important signaling molecule, an antioxidant, and performs a number of other bodily processes. It is predominantly produced in the brain by a gland called the pineal and is renowned for its involvement in sleep cycle regulation. Melatonin, on the other hand, is produced in various parts of the body, such as the eyes, body skin, platelet count, immune cells, bone marrow, mitochondria, and the gu t.

Melatonin has significance in a variety of biological processes aside from sleep control. It has an impact on the state of mind, body mass, formation of bones, immune cell activity, hormone levels, cardiovascular and vascular health, the circadian rhythm, neurological activity, and mitochondrial function. Melatonin's wide engagement in different cellular and physiological functions emphasizes its importance for general health and well-being. Melatonin has shown promise for promoting lung health when applied to the respiratory system.

According to research, the stimulation of mitochondrial function by melatonin may boost the production of energy in the lungs. Because the lungs are highly oxygenated organs, they are prone to oxidative stress. The mitochondria, which are found within the lungs, might become impaired during periods of infection, allergies, or toxicity exposure. The lungs and their local mitochondria have to coordinate antioxidant defenses to protect themselves against these potential threats. Melatonin's high antioxidant qualities can aid in the defense against oxidative stress and potentially reduce lung damage. Melatonin's significance in lung health is also supported by the presence of both melatonin transporters and receptors in most cells, including lung cells. Melatonin can be produced by mitochondria inside cells, including lung mitochondria. This emphasizes the role of melatonin in promoting lung health as well as providing antioxidant protection in the lungs' highly oxygenated environment.

Many studies have demonstrated that boosting melatonin levels may promote lung health. In one study involving mice, researchers found that melatonin administration enhanced mitochondrial function, decreased oxidative stress, and repaired lung tissues after administering a lung-compromising substance. This shows that melatonin may be able to revive the lungs and minimize the harm caused to them by oxidative stress.

Melatonin, along with its antioxidant effects, may have a role in sustaining the health of the lungs during times of illness. Lung infections frequently elicit an immunological response that includes the release of pro-inflammatory cytokines. Excessive cytokine production, on the other hand, might result in an overactive immune response that harms lung health. It has been demonstrated that melatonin can reduce the levels of several pro-inflammatory cytokines, indicating that it has the capacity to control the immunological response and promote lung vitality.

Melatonin has also been researched for its potential advantages in treating a number of respiratory diseases, including COVID-19 and chronic obstructive pulmonary disease, also known as COPD, pulmonary fibrosis, and non-small cell lung cancer (NSCLC). Melatonin supplementation has been shown in studies to be generally safe and well tolerated, even at large doses. However, more research is required to completely understand the underlying mechanisms and determine the appropriate dosage and therapy duration for various respiratory disorders. Overall, melatonin supplementation shows potential as an additional therapy for respiratory tract health. Its antioxidant characteristics, capacity to promote the functioning of mitochondria, and potential for influencing immunological responses make it an intriguing topic of study.

Benefits of Continuous Positive Airway Pressure (CPAP)

Continuous Positive Airway Pressure (CPAP) is a proven method of treating obstructive sleep apnea (OSA) and various sleep-related breathing disorders. It entails the installation of a machine that supplies a consistent flow of air under pressure through an air mask worn while sleeping, guaranteeing an unobstructed airway and undisturbed breathing.

The beneficial effects of CPAP are numerous. For starters, it alleviates OSA symptoms such as loud snoring, pauses in breathing during sleep, and excessive daytime tiredness. By keeping the airway open, CPAP avoids neck muscular collapse and allows for continuous, steady breathing through the night. Moreover, CPAP has been shown to be beneficial for cardiovascular health. High blood pressure, cardiovascular disease, and stroke are all linked to OSA. CPAP may lower blood pressure, reduce heart stress, and lessen the probability of heart disease by treating OSA and enhancing oxygenation.

In addition to its health benefits in preventing sleep apnea, CPAP is also used in the treatment of respiratory distress, especially COVID-19. It can maintain lung function and improve oxygenation by providing continuous elevated pressure to the airways. However, it is important to emphasize that the use of CPAP in COVID-19 cases should be decided individually by medical professionals.

In summary, CPAP is a very successful therapy for sleep-disordered breathing, such as OSA, and improves cardiovascular health. It has been used to treat respiratory distress, especially in COVID-19 cases, showing how versatile and effective it is in promoting respiratory health.

Benefits of Hyperbaric Oxygen Therapy (HBOT)

Hyperbaric Oxygen Therapy (HBOT) offers a variety of benefits. First and foremost, it accelerates wound healing by promoting cell regeneration and collagen synthesis, thus supporting chronic wounds and recovery after surgery. In addition, HBOT supports neurological rehabilitation by promoting tissue repair and neuroplasticity in conditions such as traumatic brain injury and stroke.

The anti-inflammatory properties of HBOT relieve discomfort and swelling and prove valuable in the treatment of chronic inflammatory diseases. Its role in optimizing the immune response and tissue oxygenation strengthens the body's defenses against infection and revitalizes cellular processes.

In emergencies, HBOT quickly helps with carbon monoxide poisoning and supports healing after surgical procedures by accelerating wound healing and reducing the risk of infection. The impressive versatility of HBOT is also evident in the treatment of respiratory disorders, as in select cases with COVID-19. This adaptability underscores the importance of HBOT in a variety of medical contexts and makes it a robust and invaluable therapeutic avenue.

Ozone Therapy

Ozone therapy is a complementary medicine treatment that involves injecting ozone gas into the patient's body to enhance healing and overall well-being. The use of ozone, an intensely reactive form of oxygen, is being pursued due to its possible therapeutic benefits. One of the most significant advantages of treatment with ozone is its antimicrobial characteristics. Ozone has been shown to successfully kill viruses, fungi, bacteria, and other diseases. Ozone therapy can aid the body's immune system and fight diseases by targeting and killing these infectious agents.

Moreover, ozone therapy has the potential to improve the body's oxygenation and circulation. When ozone is delivered into the bloodstream, it can boost oxygen delivery to tissues, increasing cellular activity and boosting healing. Increased blood circulation can also help with nutrition delivery and waste disposal, which can benefit overall well-being and energy levels. One of the most effective treatments for increasing blood oxygen levels is intravenous ozone therapy, especially major autohemotherapy. During this operation, a small portion of the patient's plasma is taken, treated using ozone, and then injected right back into their bloodstream via an IV.

Ozone therapy showed potential in the treatment of a variety of illnesses. It's been used to help control chronic ailments like Lyme's disease, severe fatigue, and autoimmune disorders. Furthermore, the use of ozone therapy is being studied for its possible applications in healing wounds, alleviating pain, and even as an adjuvant treatment for certain forms of cancer. However, while utilizing ozone therapy to treat respiratory disorders, precautions must be taken because inadvertent ozone intake might significantly increase lung irritation or harm. To maintain protection and prevent any unwanted occurrences associated with ozone gas exposure, it is critical to receive ozone treatment under the instruction of a certified specialist.

Finally, ozone treatment serves as a complementary and different method that attempts to promote health through the injection of ozone gas. Its possible benefits include antibacterial properties, higher levels of oxygen and blood circulation, and support for a variety of health issues. However, more research is required in order to clarify the mechanism of action and evaluate its efficacy in treating certain medical disorders.

Infrared Therapy and Infrared Sauna Benefits for Your Lungs

Infrared treatments and infrared sauna sessions are attracting a lot of interest because of their potential lung health advantages. Infrared light waves are used in these methods to produce heat that penetrates deeper inside the body, providing a variety of therapeutic effects. Improved blood circulation is one of the most significant advantages of infrared therapy and infrared sauna sessions for the lungs. Infrared radiation generates heat, which dilates blood vessels and improves the flow of blood through the entire body, especially the lungs. Increased blood circulation can improve oxygen supply to lung tissues, promoting respiratory performance and general lung health.

In addition to improving circulation, infrared therapy, and sauna sessions could have anti-inflammatory qualities. Chronic lung inflammation can aggravate respiratory disorders such as asthma as well as chronic obstructive pulmonary disease (COPD). Infrared therapy and sauna sessions possess the potential to reduce symptoms while boosting lung function in people with these illnesses by lowering inflammation. Furthermore, the heat from infrared treatments and sauna sessions can help relax and widen the airways, thereby alleviating respiratory problems such as shortness of breath and congestion of the lungs. The warmth may additionally assist with relaxing and reducing stress, which could have an indirect effect on lung health because stress may hinder respiratory function.

While infrared therapy and infrared sauna sessions possess the potential to improve lung health, they shouldn't be utilized in place of standard medical treatment for respiratory diseases. These techniques can be utilized in addition to conventional medical treatment.

Chapter 5

KIDNEYS CLEANSE

The human body's capacity to effectively remove toxins and pollutants declines as we age. Our kidneys are among the most significant organs in our body and serve as our well-being regulators. These organs begin their crucial duty of cleansing our bloodstream, filtering out toxin substances, and establishing a healthy internal environment from the minute we are brought into this world. However, our kidneys face the challenge of accumulating toxins and harmful substances as time passes, affecting their performance and possibly endangering our health. Adopting the kidney cleanse journey is necessary to revive and renew these filters, maintain our general health, and promote longevity.

Our kidneys act as filters; they are constantly working to cleanse our bloodstream by removing waste and impurities to help maintain the purity and functionality of our organs. Moreover, our kidneys play a primary role in regulating our blood pressure. They produce renin, which helps control salt and water balance and blood pressure and lowers the possibility of hypertension-related illnesses. These remarkable and important organs additionally perform a key function in regulating the equilibrium of critical nutrients such as phosphate, sodium, and calcium, which increases bone mass and strength. Furthermore, they support the cardiovascular system and preserve a healthy heart rhythm by carefully monitoring potassium levels.

In addition to physical health, the kidneys also impact our mental and emotional well-being. They influence brain activity, feelings of anxiety, and behavior. By maintaining an intricate balance of important components, they promote calm, mental well-being, and healthy behavior patterns.

The hidden strength of the kidneys, however, is their ability to increase vitality through the production of red blood cells. They improve physical fitness and mental clarity by increasing oxygenation through increased red blood cell production. In addition, the kidneys activate vitamin D, which supports the immune system, bone density, and overall vitality of the body.

As we embark on our kidney cleansing, we should keep in mind that our kidneys are not ordinary organs. They are force multipliers that help us stay healthy and alert by performing a number of functions. Through kidney cleansing, we will learn simple but effective methods to nourish and revitalize our kidneys in harmony with our pursuit of a longer, healthier, and happier life.

What a Renal or Kidney Cleanse Will Improve

A renal or kidney cleanse has the potential to improve our entire well-being by addressing certain areas that can considerably improve our health and energy. This cleanse can have a transforming influence on our entire physiological functioning by cleansing and restoring the kidneys.

Lumbar pain, which is most commonly felt in the lower back, can be a continuous source of discomfort that interferes with our everyday activities. A renal cleanse is a detoxifying and regeneration treatment that successfully removes impurities and toxins that may lead to lumbar discomfort. This cleanse has the ability to treat pain in the lumbar region by establishing balance and harmony inside our kidneys, providing comfort and relief from the burden.

A kidney cleanse might also help to reduce body edema. Edema, or the accumulation of extra fluid in various regions of the human body, may result in swelling and discomfort. When our kidneys aren't working properly, fluid control might become un-balanced, resulting in edema. We begin a process of cleansing and renewing the kidneys by taking part in a renal cleanse, allowing the kidneys to restore their ability to control fluid balance effectively. As a result, bodily edema can be reduced, resulting in a feeling of lightness and better physical well-being. Aside from these regional benefits, a renal or kidney cleansing might boost our body's important func-tions. For starters, it improves blood circulation and toxin removal. The kidneys are responsible for fil-tering waste, toxic substances, and pollutants from the circulatory system. We help the kidneys optimize their filtering mechanisms by performing a renal cleanse, leading to a healthier and cleaner internal environment.

We can indirectly help cleanse the circulatory sys-tem by cleansing the kidneys. This process helps the body maintain fluid and electrolyte balance, controls blood pressure, and eliminates metabolic waste products. The kidneys perform an important function in adequately filtering blood, which helps to maintain the overall wellness of the circulatory system as a whole. As a result of the increased blood flow, the kidneys receive greater oxygenation, thus improving their performance.

Renin production, which serves to regulate blood pressure, is another important function that a kidney cleanse regulates. Renin, an enzyme produced by the kidneys, participates in the maintenance of the levels of electrolytes and fluids in the body. By performing a renal cleanse, we help the kidneys increase renin production, supporting improved blood pressure stability and lowering the chance of hypertension-related problems.

A kidney cleanse improves the balance of vital minerals, including calcium and phosphorus. The kidneys perform an important function in managing the mineral balance in the human body. A renal cleanse promotes stronger and more healthy bones by regulating this state of equilibrium, increasing bone density, and lowering the probability of skeletal problems. Furthermore, a renal or kidney cleanse maintains potassium levels in the body, supporting an appropriate heart rhythm. The kidneys play a key role in maintaining potassium homeostasis, which is crucial for heart health. The risk of rhythm abnormalities and other cardiovascular diseases can be reduced by enhancing potassium management with a renal cleanse.

A renal cleanse can also impact the relationship between the renal system and brain function. The intricate interaction between both the kidneys and the brain could have an impact on mental health, levels of anxiety, and behavioral patterns. A renal cleanse restores the proper balance of vital substances, which may result in heightened mental activity, lower anxiety levels, and better-controlled behavior, which notably decreases when experiencing severe carbohydrate cravings. Moreover, a kidney cleanse encourages the production of red blood cells, resulting in improved circulation throughout the body. This leads to increased physical performance and vitality. A kidney cleanse also promotes the synthesis of vitamin D in the body, which is necessary for the body's immune function and bone health.

We prioritize kidney function optimization and support the proper functioning of numerous bodily systems through participation in a renal or kidney cleanse. While the kidney cleanse delivers immediate benefits and ensures our kidney's harmonious functioning, this may also indirectly promote lifespan and longevity. Accepting the transforming impacts of a kidney cleanse gives us a fresh sense of vitality, increased mental and physical wellness, and a basis for long-term wellness maintenance.

Advantages of Kidney Cleanse and Disadvantages of Neglecting Kidney Cleanse

The advantages of kidney cleansing are as follows:

- Preventing Kidney Stones: Cleansing assists in reducing the chance of creating kidney stones by draining out accumulations of minerals and other substances that could result in stone formation.

- Body Detoxification: By extracting toxic substances and waste products, kidney cleansing improves the body's natural detoxifying process, supporting overall health.

- Blood Pressure Management: A properly functioning and clean kidney is capable of controlling blood pressure more effectively, lowering the likelihood of hypertension.

- Enhanced Urinary Tract Health: Kidney cleansing is beneficial to the whole urinary system, avoiding infections and enhancing urinary tract health.

The disadvantages of neglecting kidney cleansing and leaving them unclean can result in serious illnesses, as shown below:

- Reduced Kidney Function: Toxin and waste buildup may interfere with the functioning of the kidneys, leading to renal disease or failure.

- Kidney Stones: Kidney stones are particularly prone to form without frequent cleansing, causing pain and potentially serious health issues.

- Hypertension: Abnormal kidney function may lead to hypertension, putting a load on the cardiovascular system.

- Urinary Tract Infections: Poorly cleaned kidneys can result in recurring urinary tract infections, compromising bladder and kidney health.

When Should I Perform a Kidney Cleanse: Before Liver and Other Cleanses and After?

When embarking on an exhaustive cleansing process, the proper sequence and timing of several cleanses are critical to optimizing their effectiveness. When to undertake a kidney cleanse in conjunction with the liver cleanse, and other cleanses is a vital decision. Let's explore the most effective way to improve the entire detoxification process.

Carrying out a kidney cleanse prior to a liver or other cleanse can be an effective plan of action.

The kidneys act as major filters in the bloodstream, eliminating waste products and toxic materials. By starting your cleansing regimen with a kidney cleanse, you lay a solid foundation for removing toxins and encouraging proper kidney function. By initiating the kidney cleanse, you are preparing your kidneys to withstand the greater toxin load that may be discharged during successive cleanses. As the kidneys have a greater capacity to handle and remove toxins from the body, this lays the foundation for more efficient detoxification.

Having a kidney cleanse before a liver cleanse or other cleansing also helps to avoid any issues that may develop when toxins are transferred into the kidneys while they are not functioning optimally. By prioritizing kidney health, you lower the possibility of overburdening these essential organs and encourage a more efficient detoxification process. It is critical to give the body time to acclimatize after completing the kidney cleanse in order to ensure the kidneys can continue to operate efficiently. This time period allows the kidneys to recuperate and preserve their newfound health. During this time, it is best to focus on maintaining kidney health by being hydrated, eating a well-balanced diet, and making decisions that foster your general health.

After a proper interval, you can begin liver and other cleanses. The increased kidney function from the previous cleansing will synergize with the subsequent cleanses, creating a more effective and thorough detoxification process. The kidneys will collaborate with the liver to filter and remove toxins from the body, thereby improving general detoxification and rejuvenation. Individual circumstances may differ, so it is important to check with a healthcare expert. They can provide individualized advice based on your specific health demands and assist in determining the best sequence and timing of cleanses according to your specific scenario.

Remember that the purpose of a cleansing process is to help with the body's natural detoxifying processes and enhance your overall well-being. By arranging kidney cleanses before liver and other cleanses, you may maximize the benefits and provide the necessary conditions for a successful and transforming cleansing experience.

How to Perform It?

According to La Rosa (2017), the kidney cleanse entails consuming a variety of extremely depurative herbal infusions as well as supplements that enhance kidney health. Ideally, you would drink a total of five distinct herbal infusions throughout the period of three days, along with plenty of purified, pure water. While a liquid meal is preferred throughout this depuration phase, it is not always obligatory.

Herbal infusions used in this cleansing may contain uva ursi, hydrangea, altea, parsley, gravel root, nettle, rompepiedras, yerba meona, burdock, dandelion tea, red clover, goldenrod, juniper, marshmallow root, burdock root, and nettles. These herbs are well-known for their purifying effects and ability to support renal function.

It is critical to remember that this type of cleanse should be undertaken under the supervision and advice of a physician or naturopathic doctor. They can provide precise recommendations, provide dose instructions, and confirm whether the cleansing is appropriate and secure for your specific requirements. Throughout the cleanse, pay close attention to your body's signals and adapt as required. Hydration and self-care are vital during this phase.

Meals and Other Tips to Help Keep Your Kidneys Clean

Keeping your kidneys clean and healthy is essential for your overall health. Aside from particular cleansing initiatives, including kidney-friendly foods and implementing certain lifestyle choices can help promote good kidney function. Listed below are some foods and suggestions that will help keep your kidneys clean:

1. Eat a well-balanced diet rich in nutri-

ent-dense foods. Include fresh vegetables and fruits, whole grain foods, protein-packed foods, and nutritious fats in your daily diet. This maintains a sufficient supply of necessary nutrients while reducing the strain on your kidneys.

2. If you have a history of renal failure or poor kidney function, you may need to reduce phosphorus-rich foods such as dairy products, nuts, and processed animal products. To determine the optimal phosphorus consumption for your unique needs, consult a healthcare provider or a qualified dietitian.

3. Maintain appropriate blood pressure levels, as excessive blood pressure can cause kidney damage over time. Reduce sodium intake, limit drinking alcohol, eliminate smoking, participate in regular physical activity, and properly manage stress.

4. Consuming berries, such as blueberries, strawberries, and raspberries, is high in antioxidants. They supply vital nutrients while also boosting kidney health.

5. Include fresh citrus fruits in your diet, such as limes, lemons, and oranges. They are high in the antioxidants vitamin C and citric acid, both of which can help prevent the produc-

tion of kidney stones.

In addition to implementing kidney-friendly foods and lifestyle decisions, there are various simple techniques to cleanse and improve the health of your kidneys. Let us examine a few of the following approaches:

- Apple Cider Vinegar: This protects against oxidative stress, regulates blood sugar levels, and dissolves stone buildup in the kidneys.

- Dates: Soaking and eating them dissolve and flush out kidney stones, and their fiber content lowers the chance of stone formation.

- Pomegranate: High in potassium, it eliminates toxins from the body, prevents the formation of stones, and reduces urine acidity.

- Basil: Basil is a natural diuretic that improves kidney function, lowers urinary acid levels, and aids in the breakdown of kidney stones.

These approaches, as well as cucumber juice, beets, coconut water, and cherries, help to maintain your overall kidney health. Additionally, maintaining a well-balanced and diverse diet and staying hydrated by drinking plenty of water during the day can go a long way for your kidneys. Not to mention, having a routine of physical activity and reducing stress levels can also improve the overall health of your kidneys.

Daily Routine: An Easy-to-Follow Plan for Kidney Cleanse

- Hydration is crucial for kidney health, and studies show that hydration status and fluid intake have a clear association with body composition and weight.

- To support kidney health, limit sodium intake to avoid straining the kidneys and contributing to high blood pressure.

- Ensure the water you drink has the right osmolality (appropriate balance of salts) to prevent dehydration. Some bottled water may reduce water salts during treatment, impacting its hydrating properties. Opt for water with the appropriate mineral content, and consider using filtered tap water whenever possible.

- Engage in regular, moderate physical activity to improve blood circulation and support kidney function.

- Quit smoking and limit alcohol consumption, as they can be detrimental to kidney health.

- Manage stress through techniques like meditation, yoga, or deep breathing exercises, as chronic stress can negatively affect the kidneys.

In-Depth Kidney Cleanse Plan 1: Herbal Kidney Cleanse

Duration: 7 days

- Hydration: Drink plenty of water throughout the day to effectively flush out toxins.

- Dandelion Root Tea: Consume dandelion root tea twice a day; known for its diuretic properties that aid kidney cleansing.

- Nettle Leaf Tea: Drink nettle leaf tea daily to support kidney function and waste elimination.

- Cranberry Juice: Have a glass of diluted, unsweetened cranberry juice daily to promote kidney health and prevent urinary tract infections.

- Kidney-Cleansing Smoothie: Prepare a kidney-cleansing smoothie with ingredients like cucumber, lemon, parsley, and watermelon, known for their kidney-friendly properties.

In-Depth Kidney Cleanse Plan 2: Juice Cleanse

Duration: 3 days

Note: Before starting a juice cleanse, consult a healthcare professional, especially if you have any medical conditions or take medications.

- Fresh Vegetable Juices: Consume fresh vegetable juices throughout the day, including ingredients like cucumber, celery, carrots, beets, and leafy greens, known for their benefits to kidney health.

- Lemon Water: Begin your day with warm lemon water to promote hydration and support kidney function.

- Herbal Tea: Sip on herbal teas like dandelion root, nettle leaf, or ginger tea during the cleanse to aid kidney detoxification.

- Watermelon Flush: On the second day, have a watermelon flush, consuming only watermelon for one full day. Watermelon is a natural diuretic and helps cleanse the kidneys.

Reintroduction Phase: On the third day, gradually reintroduce solid foods into your diet, starting with light and kidney-friendly meals like steamed vegetables and quinoa.

Chapter 6

LYMPHATIC SYSTEM CLEANSE

Within the complex fabric of the human body is a unique system defined as the lymphatic system—a combination of tissues, veins, and organs that quietly plays a key role in sustaining our general wellness and a healthy lifestyle. Lymphatic tissue is an essential element of the body's lymphatic system, providing the foundation for its intricate structure. This tissue, which is made up of specific cells and structures, is crucial in storing and maintaining lymphocytes, or immune cells, that protect our systems from harmful diseases and external invaders.

As we delve further, we come across many forms of lymphatic tissue, all of which have their own set of traits and functions. Lymph nodes, which are little bean-shaped structures that are strategically distributed through the body, serve as key checks, screening, and purifying lymph fluid as it moves through. Immune cells congregate at these nodes in the body, where they interact with one another and recognize and defend against harmful microbes. The spleen, another important lymphatic organ, serves as a blood reserve and a place for the recycling of damaged or old blood cells.

The lymphatic system must be activated in order to work properly, and lymphatic cleansing is vital in this regard. Exercise appears to be a potent stimulant in this aspect. Physical exercise causes muscle contractions, which promote lymphatic fluid circulation through the body. By walking, running, or practicing Pilates inverted postures, we can harness the force of gravity to aid lymph drainage and circulation. We support the evacuation of toxic substances, waste products, and extra fluids through these activities, improving the general efficiency of the immune system as a whole.

Aside from exercise, a variety of complementary therapies and self-care routines can help stimulate and maintain the lymphatic system. Alternative treatments that use gentle, rhythmic motions that stimulate lymph flow, relieve congestion, and improve detoxification include manual lymphatic drainage, ozone therapy, and various kinds of massage. Furthermore, methods such as both warm and cold showers, breathing deeply, dry brushing, and eating foods that stimulate lymph flow may help unblock and unclog the lymphatic system.

In this chapter, we'll go on a fascinating journey through the lymphatic system cleanse, unraveling its complicated functions and providing light on how we might improve its functionality. Understanding the importance of this critical tissue and adopting ways to stimulate and cleanse the lymphatic system can pave the way for improved immunological responses, better health, and a higher sense of vitality in every aspect of our lives.

What Is the Lymphatic System?

The lymphatic system is a complex and sophisticated network of tissues, veins, and organs that plays an important role in the general wellness and health of the body. The lymphatic system, sometimes known as the human body's "second circulatory system," works in tandem with the blood circulatory system in order to guarantee adequate fluid balance, immunological function, and waste elimination.

Lymphatic vessels, which look similar to the vessels of the blood but transport a transparent liquid known as lymph instead of blood, are located in the heart of the lymphatic system. Lymph is made up of water, proteins, lipids, immune cells, and waste products from cells. These vessels connect to form a vast network that runs through the body, touching almost every organ and tissue, including superficial and deep tissues. The lymphatic system's principal job is to accumulate and convey lymph fluid. This fluid is produced in the gaps between the cells, where it facilitates the delivery of nutrients, oxygen, and hormones. As lymph travels throughout the connective tissues, it gathers waste, surplus fluid, and cell debris, acting as the human body's drainage system.

In order to ease the passage of lymph, lymphatic vessels are outfitted with single-way valves, which enable fluid to travel in one specific direction—toward the heart. As lymphatic vessels congregate, they form bigger vessels known as lymphatic trunks, which eventually unite to produce two significant lymphatic ducts: the right lymphatic duct and the thoracic duct. These ducts subsequently drain the lymph into the circulation near the neck.

Lymph nodes are small, bean-shaped structures found along lymphatic vessels and in critical sites across the body. Lymph nodes serve as filters, capturing and removing foreign particles such as viruses, bacteria, and cancer cells. To guard against these potential threats, specialist immune system cells, known as lymphocytes, launch immune system responses within the lymph nodes. Lymph nodes are especially concentrated in the armpits, neck, and groin.

Apart from these lymph nodes, the lymphatic system comprises other vital organs that aid in immunological function. The spleen, which is found in the upper left abdomen, functions as a blood filter, eliminating damaged or old red blood cells and retaining immune cells. The thymus gland, located behind the breastbone in the chest, is in charge of the maturation and growth of T lymphocytes, a kind of white blood cell. Tonsils and adenoids, which are found in the throat and nose passageways, respectively, act as defensive systems, trapping and eliminating infections that enter the human body via respiratory and oral pathways. The lymphatic system is also responsible for delivering nutritional fats and vitamins that are fat-soluble from the gut to the bloodstream. Lacteals, which are small projections in the colon, absorb these lipids and transfer them in the form of chyle—a milky fluid—through lymphatic vessels to the circulation, which is where they are used by the body for many different purposes.

To summarize, the lymphatic system is a complicated network that supports the human body's general wellness and immunity. The lymphatic system assists in preserving fluid balance, eliminating toxins and waste products, protecting against infections, and playing a role in the absorption of dietary lipids by collecting and moving fluid from the lymph system, purifying it using the lymph nodes, and coordinating immune system responses. Learning the lymphatic system's importance and how it works is essential for recognizing the body's intricate self-defense mechanisms and sustaining optimum health.

Benefits of a Healthy Lymphatic System

A healthy, functioning lymphatic system provides an array of perks that enhance general well-being. The improved state of the immune system's performance is one of the main benefits. Using both lymph nodes and immune system cells, the lymphatic system is a key component of the body's protection against ailments and infections. The capacity of these immune system elements to detect and eliminate harmful infections, viruses, bacteria, and erroneous cells is improved by maintaining an optimal lymphatic system. This enhanced immune response can protect your well-being and lower your probability of contracting certain diseases.

A strong lymphatic system not only supports the body's immune system but also helps to lessen edema and inflammation. Inflammation arises when tissues are harmed or infected as a form of defense against infection. However, if inflammation continues or develops into a chronic condition, it may result in pain, discomfort, and tissue injury. By eliminating extra fluid and waste from the afflicted areas, the lymphatic system plays an important role in controlling inflammation. The lymphatic system contributes to reducing inflammation, reducing swelling, and promoting tissue regeneration by playing a draining role.

Digestion and nutrition absorption are both affected by a healthy lymphatic system, which is another important advantage. Dietary lipids and fat-soluble vitamins are transported via lacteals, specialized lymphatic capillaries found in the digestive tract. These nutrients are necessary for many body processes, including the synthesis of hormones, the growth of cells, and energy balance. The effective breakdown of these nutrients into the bloodstream from the intestinal tract takes place when the lymph system is operating at its peak, enabling good nutrition as well as promoting general health.

Cleansing the lymphatic system can indirectly contribute to the cleansing of both deep and superficial tissues. The lymphatic system plays a vital role in removing waste products, toxins, and excess fluid from tissues, promoting their overall health and function.

Here are examples of deep and superficial tissues that can benefit from a well-functioning lymphatic system:

- Deep tissues: Muscles, Fascia, Nerves, Blood

vessels, Ligaments, Organs, Deep connective tissues, and bones

- Superficial tissues: Skin, Hair follicles, Subcutaneous tissue, Superficial veins, Superficial nerves, and superficial fascia

The promotion of longevity can also be promoted by having a healthy lymphatic system. A healthy lymphatic system supports the immune system, lowers chronic inflammation, and enhances the absorption of nutrients, all of which contribute to the body's equilibrium and peak efficiency. By eliminating waste products and toxins from tissues and cells, it helps with the detoxification process. In addition to promoting longevity, this cleansing action lowers the likelihood of contracting chronic diseases linked to toxic accumulation and compromised immune system responses.

Signs of a Clogged Lymphatic System

Numerous symptoms could indicate a clogged lymphatic system. The following are some warning signs to keep an eye out for:

1. Swollen lymph nodes: Particularly those situated in the neck region, the armpits, and the groin, could represent an indication of lymphatic congestion. They may also be tender and painful.

2. Fatigue and Lethargy: Having a clogged lymphatic system could be the reason why you feel perpetually exhausted, lethargic, and low on energy even after getting enough rest.

3. Digestive Issues: Congestion of the lymphatic system can result in bloating, diarrhea, constipation, indigestion, and food allergies.

4. Skin Problems: Acne, eczema, rashes, dryness, and itching could be signs of toxins building up and impaired lymphatic function.

How to Cleanse and Support the Lymphatic System

The lymphatic system is essential to the system's detoxification process because it is in charge of expelling toxic substances and waste products from the body. When the lymph system is working effectively, it facilitates the removal of waste and toxins from the human body, which is helpful in avoiding the buildup of toxic substances that may cause chronic diseases and other medical conditions. Toxins can still be removed from the body, although the lymphatic system may be less efficient if it becomes clogged or overwhelmed. As a result, toxins may accumulate in the body, increasing the risk of oxidative stress-related illnesses, chronic inflammation, and other conditions that shorten your lifespan.

The lymphatic system can benefit from cleansing to increase longevity. A strong immune system is necessary for warding off infections and illnesses that can decrease lifespan, and the lymphatic system plays a vital role in ensuring that this immune system is in optimal condition. Chronic inflammation has been linked to a range of health problems, including cancer, heart disease, and Alzheimer's disease, as a result of a clogged lymphatic system.

By cleansing your lymphatic system, you could help in the removal of toxic substances and waste from your body, which may improve general health and longevity. There are various techniques for detoxing the lymph system, such as exercise and movement, dry brushing, therapeutic massage, and herbal remedies.

- Exercise and Movement: One of the most effective methods to cleanse the lymphatic system is exercise. Regular exercise causes your muscles to relax and contract, resulting in an improvement in the movement of lymphatic fluid throughout your body. This may encourage the flow of lymph and enhance the body's capacity to eliminate waste and harmful substances.

- Dry brushing: Dry brushing involves gently massaging the skin with a natural bristle brush. This can help increase lymphatic flow and enhance the body's capacity to eliminate toxic substances and waste products.

- Massage therapy: The lymphatic system can greatly benefit from massage therapy in terms of cleansing and support. Methods like manual lymphatic drainage (MLD) put the emphasis on slow, rhythmic movements that encourage lymph flow and relieve congestion.

- Herbal medicine: The lymphatic system can be maintained and cleansed with the use of specific herbs and nutritional supplements. Burdock root, red clover, dandelion root, and turmeric are a few examples. These plants have cleansing and anti-inflammatory qualities that may be beneficial for cleansing lymphatic congestion.

Here Are Three Main Techniques to Help Unclog the Lymphatic System

1. Exercise: Exercise serves as one of the most effective approaches to unclogging the lymphatic system. Your muscles contract and relax during physical activity, creating a

pumping motion that helps lymphatic fluid move around the body. The system is able to effectively clear toxins and waste items thanks to the increased movement that increases lymphatic flow. Even though all forms of physical activity have their advantages, leaping or bouncing exercises like jump jacks or rebound are particularly good at promoting lymphatic drainage.

2. Dry Brushing: A highly effective method for unclogging the lymphatic system is dry brushing. The act of dry brushing promotes the lymphatic vessels that are located just below the skin's surface by gently stroking the outermost layer of skin using an all-natural bristle brush. The body's ability to rid itself of waste and toxins is improved by this stimulation, which stimulates lymphatic drainage. To dry brush efficiently, begin at your feet and brush upward with long, sweeping strokes toward your heart. Every part of your body should be brushed several times, with your armpits, groin, and neck being particularly important because they are areas where there are lots of lymph nodes. But you must be very careful not to brush over any rashes or patches of broken skin.

3. Message Therapy: Massage treatment is an

excellent method for unclogging the lymph system. The removal of waste materials and toxins is made easier when pressure is applied to the skin and supporting muscles. Deep tissue massage and lymphatic drainage massage are two of the best massage methods available for lymphatic drainage.

Here Are Seven Alternative Therapies for Cleansing the Lymphatic System

1. Rebounding: Rebounding is a form of physical activity that involves jumping on a small trampoline. This method has the potential to help lymphatic flow, which facilitates the body's removal of waste products and harmful substances. Rebounding may also promote improved circulation and reduce inflammation.

2. Infrared Sauna: Infrared saunas use infrared light to heat the body, resulting in increased lymphatic flow and better detoxification of toxic substances and waste products. These saunas are also well known for their ability to improve circulation and reduce inflammation.

3. Manual Lymphatic Drainage: The purpose of the specialized massage method known as

manual lymphatic drainage is to increase the body's capacity to naturally eliminate waste products and toxins by promoting lymphatic flow. It is a useful strategy for enhancing lymphatic health and detoxifying procedures.

4. Acupuncture: Acupuncture is a form of traditional Chinese medicine that involves inserting tiny needles into particular body sites. This technique has been proven to be successful at boosting lymphatic flow and the body's ability to rid itself of waste and toxins. Acupuncture has also demonstrated effectiveness in lowering inflammation and enhancing immune system performance. This therapy seeks to regain balance and advance overall health by concentrating on particular acupuncture points.

5. Cupping Therapy: Cupping therapy is an approach that uses suction cups to increase lymphatic drainage and improve circulation. The cups gently raise the skin by creating a suction effect, which encourages lymph fluid movement and enhances the flow of blood in the area that is being treated. This method can help detoxify the body's processes and maintain lymphatic health. Numerous advantages of cupping therapy include easing

discomfort, easing muscle tension, and enhancing overall health.

6. Yoga: Yoga is a healthy physical activity that can successfully boost lymphatic flow and improve the body's inherent capacity to rid itself of toxins and waste. Yoga movements like shoulder stands and downward dogs are particularly good for promoting lymphatic function. Inversions and moderate compression of particular body parts are used in these poses, which can increase lymphatic drainage and aid in detoxification. Yoga can help you maintain an optimal lymphatic system and improve your general state of health.

7. Epsom Salt Bath: Sulfate and magnesium are the two main components of Epsom salt, and when combined, they contribute to detoxification and the removal of toxins from the body. Epsom salt baths are a common alternative therapy for detoxifying the lymphatic system. By bathing in warm bathwater with Epsom salt, the magnesium sulfate that's contained in the salt may help with lymphatic flow and detoxing. This treatment is said to help the body remove toxic substances and contaminants, as well as minimize swelling and inflammation. Regularly

bathing in Epsom salts can be a relaxing and advantageous activity to improve lymphatic health.

Here Are Three Massage Lymphatic Drainage Techniques in Detail

1. Manual Lymphatic Drainage (MLD): The mild massage technique known as manual lymphatic drainage (MLD) was created with the goal of enhancing the body's capacity to cleanse itself of harmful substances and waste products by stimulating the flow of lymphatic fluid. A trained massage therapist uses gentle, rhythmic strokes in an MLD session to promote lymphatic fluid flow throughout the body. This technique is often used on the legs, neck, arms, and face. When it comes to lowering swelling, enhancing circulation, and promoting general lymphatic health, MLD can be very beneficial.

2. Deep-Tissue Massage: Deep-tissue massage can help with the drainage of lymphatics. To reach the deepest levels of connective and muscle tissue, a deep tissue massage therapist uses strong pressure and slow stroking motions. This focused strategy can increase the circulation of lymph and the body's ca-

pacity to rid itself of impurities and waste. Deep-tissue massage is typically utilized on the muscles of the shoulders, back, and legs. It is very useful for relieving muscle tension, increasing circulation, and promoting lymphatic health.

3. Cupping Therapy: The interesting massage technique known as "cupping therapy," which uses suction cups, is an appealing method to improve circulation and boost lymphatic motion. In a cupping session, the massage professional carefully positions the cups on the skin to create a vacuum effect that stimulates lymphatic fluid flow, which helps in the removal of waste and toxins. Frequently targeted locations for cupping therapy include the shoulders, back, and legs, where it has been shown to be effective in lowering muscle tension, boosting circulation, and fostering general lymphatic health. Cupping therapy is an effective approach to promoting the human body's own detoxification mechanisms and offers a useful route to rejuvenation and wellness.

The Most Effective Herbal Remedies for Cleansing the Lymphatic System

1. Dandelion Root: Dandelion root has been

revered for its remarkable help in preserving the health of the lymph system and liver for many years. This herb has the amazing potential to boost lymphatic flow and improve the process of detoxification because it is full of helpful substances. Additionally, dandelion root functions as a mild diuretic, assisting in the removal of harmful substances from the body. A holistic strategy for enhancing the health of your liver and fostering a robust lymphatic system is to embrace the dandelion root's natural potency.

2. Burdock Root: Burdock root, a recognized herb with a centuries-long history, is a powerful lymphatic booster. This amazing plant, which is teeming with beneficial compounds, has the power to promote lymphatic motion and support the body's detoxifying procedures. Burdock root also functions as an effective diuretic, assisting with the removal of unwanted substances from the body. The lymphatic system can be maintained, and overall vitality may be enhanced, by acknowledging the healing power of burdock root.

3. Red Clover: Red clover, which is steeped in traditional knowledge, emerges as a valued herb that has long been hailed for its

tremendous effects on lymph health and cleansing. This herb has the potential to stimulate the flow of lymph and improve the body's inherent capacity to eliminate foreign substances because it is rich in powerful compounds. Consuming the medicinal element of red clover begins a transforming journey, balancing the lymph system and reviving general wellness, providing a fresh zest for life.

4. Cleavers: The historically significant plant cleavers have gained notoriety for its tremendous effects on lymphatic health as well as detoxification. This botanical miracle, which is high in bioactive components, has a significant influence on lymphatic motion, assisting the body's efficient disposal of unwanted and toxic materials. Through utilizing the curative benefits of cleavers, people set out on a path to improving lymphatic health and fostering effective detoxification procedures. Cleavers establishes itself as a valued ally in the search for total vitality and harmonious physiological function due to its renowned reputation and scientific foundations.

5. Echinacea: The capacity of the renowned herb echinacea to strengthen immune sys-

tem function and encourage lymphatic movement has long been admired. This botanical gem, which is brimming with bioactive components, increases lymphatic drainage, assisting in the efficient elimination of unwanted substances from the human body. The healing qualities of echinacea act as an all-natural immune system booster and support lymphatic system health in general. Echinacea is a wonderful tool for fostering vitality and promoting ideal lymphatic function due to its historical relevance and research backing.

Chapter 7

Skin Cleansing

We usually focus on keeping a healthy diet, getting regular exercise, and incorporating different lifestyle habits into our quest for optimum health and longevity. However, the necessity for proper skin cleansing is one important factor that is sometimes disregarded in this endeavor. The largest organ in the body, the skin plays a vital function in our general health in addition to acting as a protective barrier. A fully integrated approach to choosing longevity requires adopting a thorough understanding of the significance of skin cleansing when it comes to the longevity and well-being of our skin.

The importance of skin cleansing is mostly found in its immediate effect on general skin health. Every day, our skin is subjected to a wide range of external variables, such as toxic substances, UV rays, pollution, and harsh chemicals. These elements, together with internal activities such as perspiration and sebum output, can result in an accumulation of debris, germs, and dead cells from the skin, causing blocked pores and other skin-related issues. We may get rid of these pollutants and keep clear, clean skin by following a regular and efficient skin-cleansing regimen. Furthermore, studies have revealed the indisputable link between longevity and skin health. Our skin is a window into our interior health, and both its texture and condition reveal important information regarding how we are doing as a whole. When our skin is damaged due to carelessness or exposure to toxic substances, it can cause irritation, premature aging of the skin, and a weaker immune response. In contrast, by placing a high priority on skin cleansing, we may counteract these detrimental effects and encourage healthy, youthful-looking skin, thus improving our lifespan and quality of life.

Moreover, effective skin cleansing affects our total physical and emotional health in addition to the quality and lifespan of our skin. We can feel touch, warmth, and pain because of the important sensory function of our skin. We may maximize these sensory processes, which will improve our body awareness and our capacity to react to external stimuli, by keeping our skin clean and healthy. In addition, following a regular skin cleansing practice can be a kind of self-care, encouraging relaxation, lowering stress levels, and improving self-confidence—all of which constitute key components in our quest for longevity.

Let's not undervalue the importance of skin cleansing as we set out on this journey to longevity by choice. We may take full advantage of the function that our skin plays in promoting longevity by realizing how crucial it is to keep a clear, healthy complexion. In this chapter, we will examine several skin cleansing techniques, learn about the research behind their efficacy, and arm ourselves with useful information and tools for enhancing the health of our skin. Let's open the door to a rich and enduring life by embracing the transforming power of appropriate skin cleansing.

Why Cleanse the Skin?

The ritual of skin cleansing emerges as a vital cornerstone in our pursuit of vibrant and healthy skin. Understanding the value of clear pores and committing to a regular skin cleansing practice can help us access a wealth of advantages that go far beyond outward appearances. Let's explore why cleansing your skin is essential for achieving ideal skin health, from enhancing a clear and beautiful complexion to bolstering the skin's natural barriers.

The first and most important factor in preserving the overall well-being of our skin is having clear pores. Our pores attract debris, extra oil, cosmetic residue, and environmental contaminants during the course of the day. These compounds can cause blockages and foster the growth of bacteria when they build up in the pores, which can result in typical skin problems, including acne, blackheads, and irritation. We may efficiently eliminate these harmful chemicals by including routine skin cleansing in every day's routine, letting our skin's pores breathe easily, and avoiding future skin issues. The skin on our bodies sheds dead cells naturally, which can build up on the outer layer and make a complexion appear dull, harsh, and lifeless. Exfoliation while cleansing gently peels away unwanted dead cells, leaving a fresh and beautiful layer of skin beneath. The skin will become smoother as a result, and its capacity to absorb healthy nutrients from skincare products will also improve.

Additionally, a thorough skin cleansing is essential for regulating oil production. Excess oil can accumulate on our skin if it is not properly washed, causing greasiness, plugged pores, and possibly outbreaks. We can establish an ideal oil balance by eliminating impurities and managing oil levels through frequent cleansing, providing a more healthy and even complexion. Furthermore, skin cleansing helps maximize the efficiency of skincare products. The active compounds found in the skin-care we use are more readily absorbed by clean, impurity-free skin. These products, whether they be moisturizers, serums, or treatments, are able to penetrate the skin more deeply and provide their intended advantages more successfully, which raises the effectiveness of the product as a whole. We get the most out of each product and get the best results when we combine thorough skin cleansing with a well-planned skincare routine.

The cleansing of the skin also delays the onset of premature aging. Our skin is subjected to external factors such as ultraviolet (UV) rays, pollution, and harmful free radicals throughout the day, which all contribute to the gradual loss of elastin and collagen, resulting in the appearance of fine lines, wrinkles, and sagging skin. We decrease the damage that these toxic chemicals can cause by rigorously cleansing and removing them, maintaining our skin's youthful glow, and fostering more resilience and a healthier complexion.

Finally, cleansing the skin is necessary for its general well-being and appeal. We may obtain a bright, radiant complexion while limiting the chance of skin disorders by keeping our pores clean, exfoliating our dead skin cells, controlling oil secretion, and enhancing the effectiveness of our skincare products. A quick yet effective step in maintaining ideal skin health is to include an extensive and consistent skin cleanse in everyday life.

Ten Skin Cleanse Techniques to Perform at Home

1. Oil cleansing method: The oil cleansing technique entails cleaning the skin with organic oils like coconut oil, jojoba oil, or almond oil. By keeping the skin moisturized and nourished, these oils assist in dissolving and removing impurities, even stubborn makeup.

2. Double cleansing: To remove oil-based substances and makeup, double cleansing involves a two-step procedure that starts with an oil-based cleanser. After that, a water-based cleanser is used to remove any leftover residue, sweat, or dirt. The skin will have a fresh and clean surface thanks to this thorough cleansing technique.

3. Exfoliation: Exfoliation is the process of removing dead skin cells from the skin in order to display a softer, brighter complexion. While chemical exfoliation uses solutions containing chemicals such as beta-hydroxy acids (BHAs) or alpha-hydroxy acids (AHAs) to break down dead skin cells, physical exfoliation uses mild scrubs or brushes.

4. Facial steaming: Warm steam is applied to

the skin during a facial steaming procedure to help the pores open up, allowing for deeper cleaning and improved product absorption. For a healthy glow, it helps to stimulate circulation, remove debris, and clear up pores.

5. Clay, charcoal, and honey masks: For removing impurities, reducing excess oil, and nourishing the skin, people often make use of clay masks, charcoal masks, and honey masks. In contrast to honey masks, which hydrate and have antibacterial characteristics, charcoal and clay masks function by detoxifying and cleansing the skin.

6. Epson salt baths: Baths with Epsom salts are not only soothing, but they also have advantages for your skin. Epsom salt's minerals help in cleansing and detoxification, as well as soothing inflammation and improving skin moisture.

7. Green tea toner: The antioxidant qualities of green tea toner, which is made from brewed green tea, are well known. It leaves the skin feeling revitalized and renewed by reducing inflammation, constricting pores, and shielding it from free radicals.

8. Witch hazel toner: Witch hazel toner origi-

nated from witch hazel shrubs and works as an astringent to remove excess oil and toxins from the skin. Additionally, it helps with pore tightening and irritation relief.

9. Apple cider vinegar toner: When combined with water, apple cider vinegar toner works to balance the pH of the skin and manage oil production. It may also possess antimicrobial qualities, making it favorable for skin that is prone to acne.

10. Aloe vera gel: Aloe vera gel is a moisturizing and calming component that can be applied as a toner or a cleanser. It is appropriate for tender or irritation-prone skin since it reduces inflammation, hydrates the skin, and speeds up recovery.

Ten Therapies Performed by Professionals to Cleanse the Skin

1. Chemical peels: In chemical peels, a chemical solution is applied to the skin, causing regulated exfoliation, and removing the top layer that contains dead skin cells. This procedure targets issues such as lines and wrinkles, uneven appearance, and hyperpigmentation while promoting cell renewal to provide young and rejuvenated skin.

2. Microdermabrasion: A device used in the non-invasive treatment of microdermabrasion that removes the topmost layer of skin. It exfoliates dead skin cells, which leaves behind smoother, healthier-looking skin. It also helps to reduce the visibility of lines and wrinkles, acne scarring, sunburn, and discoloration.

3. Laser resurfacing: The removal of damaged skin layers, stimulation of collagen synthesis, and promotion of rejuvenation of the skin are all achieved through laser resurfacing. It gives skin a smoother, younger appearance by efficiently treating signs of aging, scarring, age-related pigmentation, and uneven texture.

4. Ultrasonic cleansing: Low-frequency sound waves are used in ultrasonic cleansing to thoroughly clean the skin. It improves the product's absorption while removing impurities, extra oils, and dead skin cells. The skin is properly cleansed and revitalized after using this mild and non-invasive method.

5. High-frequency treatment: In order to treat a variety of skin issues, high-frequency treatment makes use of high-frequency equipment that delivers a mild electrical impulse. It assists in eradicating bacteria, low-

ering irritation, enhancing circulation, and enhancing the overall wellness of the skin. Skin that is prone to acne or is congested will benefit the most from this therapy.

6. Oxygen facial: A pressured oxygen facial is a revitalizing procedure that infuses the skin with nutrients, vitamins, and herbal extracts while also providing pressurized oxygen. It contributes to the skin's hydration, nourishment, and revitalization, giving it a smooth and glowing look.

7. LED light therapy: Utilizing particular light wavelengths, LED light therapy treats a variety of skin issues. Blue light specifically targets bacteria that cause acne, while red light promotes repair and collagen formation. This non-invasive procedure can enhance your entire complexion, skin firmness, and skin texture.

8. Radiofrequency treatment: During radiofrequency therapy, the deeper skin layers are heated using regulated radiofrequency radiation, which tightens the skin and promotes the formation of collagen. It improves skin elasticity, reduces wrinkles, and improves the overall tone and texture of your skin.

9. Dermaplaning: Dermaplaning is a manually

performed exfoliation procedure that utilizes a surgical blade to gently scrape away dead skin cells and vellus hair (peach fuzz). It smooths the skin and improves product absorption. This procedure can smooth out fine wrinkles, enhance skin texture, and produce a smooth surface for applying beauty or skincare products.

10. Microneedling: Microneedling involves inflicting targeted micro-injuries on the skin with small needles. This speeds up the skin's own repair mechanism and boosts the creation of collagen. It can lessen the visibility of stretch marks, wrinkles, and acne scars.

Ten Vitamins, Minerals, Fatty Acids, and Oligo Elements That Are Scientifically Proven to Be Necessary for Healthy Skin

1. Vitamin A: Essentail for skin regeneration and elasticity. It promotes the regulation of skin cell and sebum (natural oil) production, keeping the skin nourished and moisturized.

2. Vitamin E: It is a potent antioxidant that plays a role in protecting the skin from oxidative damage caused by free radicals and ultraviolet (UV) radiation.

3. Vitamin C: A powerful antioxidant that

boosts the production of collagen, which is necessary for maintaining the smoothness of the skin and reducing wrinkles and other signs of aging.

4. Vitamin D: Plays an important role in overall skin health and defense mechanisms, which can be useful in the prevention of infections and irritation.

5. Vitamin K: Assists with the coagulation of blood, protects the collagen in the skin, can help in the fading of under-eye dark circles, and promotes wound healing.

6. Zinc: An antioxidant and anti-inflammatory mineral that helps reduce inflammation, improve skin healing, sustain collagen levels, and increase the effectiveness of the immune system.

7. Selenium: An antioxidant mineral that helps shield the skin from damage from ultraviolet (UV) rays and might even assist in preventing skin cancer as well as other harmful effects on the environment.

8. Omega-3 Fatty Acids: These important fatty acids contribute to ensuring the health of the skin's own oil barrier, keeping it well-hydrated, and decreasing inflammation.

9. Omega-6 Fatty Acids: Another type of important fatty acid that enhances general skin health as well as contributes to preserving the skin's barrier function.

10. Copper: An oligo component that's useful in the production of collagen and wound repair, hence promoting healthy skin.

Always prioritize a balanced diet to improve your overall health and bring out your skin's natural radiance. Whenever it pertains to your skin's issues, don't be afraid to seek the advice of specialists who may offer the most appropriate and personalized recommendations.

Strategies for Skin Cleansing

1. Hydration: The secret to detoxifying the skin is to drink enough water. Water helps the body and skin cleanse out impurities, providing a bright and beautiful complexion.

2. Nutritious Diet: The body receives the vital nutrients it needs for the best skin wellness and toxin removal from a diet rich in vegetables, fruits, and whole grains. The natural detoxifying process of the skin is supported by these nutrient-rich foods.

3. Regular Exercise: The removal of toxins from

the skin is facilitated by regular physical exercise, which increases blood flow and circulation. Exercise also helps to maintain a healthy-looking complexion by providing oxygen and nutrients to the skin.

4. Dry Brushing: Dry brushing is the process of gently exfoliating the skin using a natural bristle brush while activating the lymphatic system. This method aids in the removal of impurities from the body while revitalizing and reviving the skin.

5. Sauna or Steam Room: Time spent in a heated sauna or steam room causes sweating and opens pores, which helps the skin release impurities. This cleansing procedure encourages a glowing, youthful complexion.

6. Clay Masks: Clay masks work well to remove toxins and impurities from the skin. They offer a thorough cleaning that leaves the skin looking refreshed and clear.

7. Chemical Peels: Professional skin exfoliation procedures called chemical peels help the body cleanse toxins by removing dead skin cells from the skin. These peels support a more radiant and youthful appearance.

8. Professional Facials: Professional facials provide a thorough method of deep cleans-

ing and toxin clearance. These procedures are customized to meet each person's unique skin demands, efficiently eliminating pollutants and restoring the skin's health and youthfulness.

It is important to acknowledge that while these techniques may play a role in the skin's ability to rid itself of toxins, nurturing an all-encompassing, health-conscious lifestyle is crucial for supporting good skin health and assisting systemic detoxification processes.

Epsom Salt Baths: A Natural Method for Skin Cleansing and Relaxation

Epsom salt, formally referred to as magnesium sulfate (MS), has been used for millennia as an herbal remedy known for its purifying effects. Epsom salt is considered to facilitate the body's detoxification process by drawing out impurities through the skin.

Epsom salt easily dissolves when added to warm water, releasing magnesium and sulfate ions into the water. The skin then absorbs these positive ions, promoting the relaxation of muscles, reducing swelling, and detoxifying. Magnesium acts as a necessary mineral that is important for many body processes, including energy production, blood pressure control, muscle and neuron function, and blood clotting. In contrast, sulfate helps the body remove toxins and maintain healthy liver function.

Epsom salt baths additionally help with relaxation and stress reduction in addition to their cleansing benefits. Magnesium offers a relaxing impact on your nervous system that promotes calmness and relaxation. To use Epsom salt, just add 1-2 cups of Epsom salt to warm water, soak for around 20–30 minutes, and repeat as needed to integrate Epsom salt into your cleansing program. In order to help the body flush out toxins, it's vital to hydrate properly by drinking lots of water prior to and after the bath.

Although Epsom salt baths are a useful detoxification aid, it is important to understand that they shouldn't serve as a substitute for medical care. It is advised to speak with your doctor before beginning any new treatments or therapies if you happen to have any current or pre-existing medical disorders.

Detox Patches for Foot-Based Cleansing to Eliminate Toxins

Detox patches, which are adhesive patches put on the soles of the feet before sleeping, are gaining popularity as a way to promote deep cleansing by removing impurities from one's body through the soles of the feet. These patches include a mixture of organic components that are believed to help in the process of detoxification, namely tourmaline, bamboo vinegar, and a variety of herbs. Although tourmaline is known to improve circulation and the flow of energy, bamboo vinegar is considered to help in the removal of pollutants. Even though the herbal ingredients can change, they frequently contain purifying substances like chamomile, ginger, and green tea.

A simple application of the patch's adhesive side to the foot's sole before bedtime is all that is required to use detox patches. In the morning, take off the patches after leaving them on for around 6 to 8 hours. Following application, the patches might turn dark or discolored, indicating the probable removal of impurities from your body.

While anecdotal data shows that detox patches are effective at boosting detoxification, there isn't any scientific proof to back up these assertions. It is critical to stress that detox patches should not be used in place of medical care. Before trying out novel remedies or treatments, those with underlying medical disorders or any health concerns should consult with their healthcare specialists.

Detox patches present an innovative notion based on toxin extraction through the feet. Although further research is needed to determine their usefulness, using such patches along with expert medical counsel may provide people with a well-rounded view of their health and future detoxifying efforts.

Step-By-Step Guide for Revitalizing With a Foot Bath Detox

Experience the beneficial effects of detoxifying from the convenience and comfort of your home using an in-home foot detox. This quick and easy technique provides a soothing way to encourage general well-being. Take the following simple actions to start your foot bath detoxification journey:

1. Fill a basin or bathtub halfway with warm water. Make sure that the water is a comfortable temperature; stay away from hot water that could irritate your skin or make you uncomfortable.

2. By applying sea salt or Epsom salts to the water, you can increase the cleansing effects. Salt promotes relaxation and helps draw out pollutants. For each gallon of water, use around 1/2 cup of salt.

3. Enhance your experience by adding herbs or essential oils to the water. Excellent choices are peppermint, lavender, or tea tree oil, which are renowned for their calming and detoxifying effects. Alternately, think about including herbs that aid with detoxification,

like chamomile or ginger.

4. Spend 20 to 30 minutes relaxing in the pool
   with your feet submerged. Relax your sens-
   es and encourage cleansing by letting warm
   water and beneficial oils do their job.

5. After the foot bath, dry your feet completely
   and apply foot lotion or a moisturizer. The
   appearance of your skin will feel refreshed
   and invigorated after receiving nourishment
   and care.

Adopt the rejuvenating foot bath cleansing experience as an essential component of your self-care practice, helping to promote relaxation and improve your overall health.

Using Activated Charcoal to Detoxify

Charcoal has become increasingly popular in recent years as a detoxifying component in a variety of goods, from facial masks to toothpaste to nutritional supplements. Among its varieties, activated charcoal sticks out as a carefully prepared variety that has had its porosity and area of coverage increased by oxygen. This distinguishes it from regular absorption and allows it to be particularly effective at adsorbing pollutants.

When ingested, activated charcoal moves through the gut while attaching to toxins and harmful substances. It actively promotes cleansing by inhibiting how they are absorbed into the circulation of the blood, which also helps to enhance the health of the gut.

When used topically, activated charcoal is effective at removing toxins and impurities from the skin. In order to properly remove pollutants and excess oil, charcoal-infused facial masks have become an increasingly common choice for skin cleansing. This process leaves the skin feeling rejuvenated and refreshed.

Moreover, it's important to understand that activated charcoal could hinder some medications from being properly absorbed. If you are already taking any medications, you should speak to your doctor before adding activated charcoal to your regimen.

In the quest for internal and exterior cleansing, activated charcoal offers a fantastic ally. Individuals may explore the advantages it offers and improve their general well-being by appropriately using its therapeutic properties under expert guidance.

Conclusion

As we reach the final pages of "The Art of Resetting Your Body," the second book in the Longevity by Choice series, we find ourselves standing at the threshold of a remarkable transformation—one that encompasses the cleansing and detoxification of vital organs such as the brain, respiratory tract, gut, liver, kidneys, lymphatic system, and skin. Throughout this journey, we have explored the profound benefits of these practices, both for promoting longevity and, equally significant, for elevating the quality of the years we are blessed to live.

Our bodies are temples of intricate design, enduring the rigors of everyday life. As we age, the accumulation of toxins, stress, and environmental influences can take a toll on our overall health and well-being. But fear not, for the wisdom contained within these pages provides a beacon of hope, illuminating the path toward renewal and revitalization.Cleansing and detoxifying our organs offer us the opportunity to shed the weight of accumulated burdens, freeing ourselves from the grip of harmful substances that hinder our body's natural functions. By engaging in this transformative process, we embark on a journey that extends far beyond physical health—it encompasses our mental and emotional well-being as well.

As you have discovered in the day-to-day plans presented here, embracing a cleansing routine need not be daunting. Instead, it becomes a labor of self-love, a gift we give ourselves to restore harmony and balance within. The deep cleansing plans offered within these chapters lay the groundwork for inner healing, setting the stage for a lifetime of wellness and vitality.

In promoting longevity, we acknowledge the preciousness of time, cherishing each moment that life bestows upon us. However, it is equally vital to recognize that longevity alone does not guarantee a fulfilling existence. It is the quality of those years that truly matters—the joy, purpose, and fulfillment that permeate every breath we take.We encourage you, dear reader, to continue this transformative journey of self-discovery and well-being by exploring the preceding volume, "The Art of Maintaining Cell Health." There, you will uncover the secrets of nurturing your body at a cellular level, laying the groundwork for a strong and resilient foundation.

And as you turn your gaze toward the future, consider venturing into the forthcoming pages of "The Art of Controlling Your Mind and Empowering Your Body." Within those chapters, you will find the keys to unlocking the full potential of your mental and physical faculties, leading you to a state of profound balance and self-mastery.

Together, these three volumes form the Longevity by Choice series—a holistic approach to living a life of abundance, wellness, and fulfillment. They are not just books but invitations to embrace a lifelong journey of self-empowerment and well-being.

In conclusion, we extend our heartfelt gratitude to you, dear reader, for joining us on this odyssey of health and self-discovery. May the knowledge and insights gained within these pages serve as guiding lights as you continue to forge a path of radiant health, inner harmony, and longevity by choice.

With immense warmth and encouragement, Zen Lee, Author of *The Art of Resetting Your Body* and the *Longevity by Choice* series.

About the Author

Zen Lee is an accomplished woman with a Bachelor's degree in Medical Science, possessing a wealth of knowledge and a boundless passion for the subject. Her studies encompass a diverse range, including the latest research in traditional medicine, alternative therapies, and ancestral life practices. Presently, she is immersed in exploring the fascinating world of hypnosis and breathing techniques, as well as their potential applications.

Drawing from her profound understanding of the human body and mind, Zen Lee has seamlessly integrated her learnings into her own life. Now, she aspires to share this invaluable knowledge with her readers, offering a simplified analysis of the natural changes that occur within our bodies over time and how our lifestyles can influence and manipulate these transformations. From molecular to cellular and organic levels, she finds excitement in understanding the intricate workings of the human form, considering both holistic and environmental aspects.

With years of dedicated research into organic anti-aging discoveries, Zen Lee has decided to compile her insights into a series of three books. Each book serves as a compilation of the most valuable and crucial information on the subject, aiming to help readers comprehend their choices and the long-term effects their lifestyle decisions may have on their overall well-being.

Residing in a serene, self-sustaining house far from the city, Zen Lee shares her life with her loving young family. She finds joy in meditation, indulges in the pleasures of reading, and embraces the satisfaction of putting knowledge into practice. Alongside her family, she cherishes the simplicity of co-existing with nature, constantly striving for self-improvement, and nurturing the profound connection between her body and mind. Her core belief lies in the importance of getting to know oneself, understanding and accepting who we are, and embracing continuous personal, spiritual, and mental growth for ultimate fulfillment.

The upcoming series of books by Zen Lee will delve into the power of the mind and the intricate rela-

tionship between the mind and body. Scientifically verified methods to break free from overthink-
ing, such as therapeutic hypnosis and transient hypofrontality, will be explored, offering readers prac-
tical tools for their benefit.

Zen Lee's work is an embodiment of her passion
for knowledge and her desire to empower others to
lead healthier, more fulfilling lives. Her writing is an
invitation to embark on a journey of self-discovery,
tapping into the inherent wisdom of the body and
the boundless potential of the mind.

With great anticipation, Zen Lee awaits the opportunity to continue sharing her transformative insights and discoveries with her cherished readers.
Join her as she guides you through the realms of
well-being, self-awareness, and profound growth.

References

8 *Easy Ways to Cleanse Your Kidneys.*
(2017, October 11). Advanced Urology Institute. https://www.advancedurologyinstitute.com
/8-easy-ways-cleanse-kidneys/

Ackerman, S. (1992). *From Chemistry to Circuitry.*
National Academies Press (US). https://www.ncbi.
nlm.nih.gov/books/NBK234149/

Aguida, B., Pooam, M., Ahmad, M., & Jourdan, N.
(2021). Infrared light therapy relieves TLR-4 dependent hyper-inflammation of the type induced
by COVID-19. *Communicative & Integrative Biology,*
14(1), 200–211. https://doi.org/10.1080/19420889.2
021.1965718

Al-Asmakh, M., Anuar, F., Zadjali, F., Rafter, J., & Pettersson, S. (2012). Gut microbial communities modulating brain development and function. *Gut Mi-*

crobes, 3(4), 366–373. https://doi.org/10.4161/gmi c.21287

American Lung Association. (2021, November 23). *Breathing Exercises | American Lung Association*. L ung.org. https://www.lung.org/lung-health-disea ses/wellness/breathing-exercises

American Lung Association. (2021, October 6). *Tips to Keep Your Lungs Healthy*. Www.lung.org . https://www.lung.org/lung-health-diseases/we llness/protecting-your-lungs

Anjum, I., Jaffery, S. S., Fayyaz, M., Samoo, Z., & Anjum, S. (2018). The Role of Vitamin D in Brain Health: A Mini Literature Review. *Cureus*, 10(7). https://doi .org/10.7759/cureus.2960

Appleton, J. (2018). The Gut-Brain Axis: Influence of Microbiota on Mood and Mental Health. *Integrative Medicine: A Clinician's Journal*, 17(4), 28–32. https://www.ncbi.nlm.nih.gov/pmc/articl es/PMC6469458/

Axe, J. (2022, August 15). *Detox Your Liver: Try My 6-Step Liver Cleanse*. Dr. Axe. https://draxe.com/ nutrition/liver-cleanse/

Balance ONE. (2018, August 8). 10 *Natural Supplements for Healthy Liver Function*. Balance ONE. https://balanceone.com/blogs/news/the-t op-supplements-to-support-liver-function

Balla, M., Merugu, G. P., Konala, V. M., Sangani, V., Kondakindi, H., Pokal, M., Gayam, V., Adapa, S., Naramala, S., & Malayala, S. V. (2020). Back to basics: review on vitamin D and respiratory viral infections including COVID-19. *Journal of Community Hospital Internal Medicine Perspectives*, 10(6), 529–536. https://doi.org/10.1080/20009666.2020.1811074

Cafasso, J. (2019, March 8). *Steam inhalation: Cold, sinuses, procedure, benefits, cough, and*. Healthline. https://www.healthline.com/health/steam-inhalation

Cait + Co. (2022, June 16). *The Benefits of Eucalyptus in Your Shower*. Cait + Co. https://www.caitandco.com/blogs/tips-and-tricks/the-benefits-of-eucalyptus-in-your-shower

Cetinkalp, S., Simsir, I. Y., & Ertek, S. (2014). Insulin resistance in brain and possible therapeutic approaches. *Current Vascular Pharmacology*, 12(4), 553–564. https://doi.org/10.2174/1570161112999140206130426

Chhc, J. L. (2020, December 9). *Brain Detox: Is It Time for a Cleanse? (Plus How to Do It)*. Dr. Axe. https://draxe.com/health/brain-detox

CPAP Machine: What It Is, How It Works, Pros & Cons. (n.d.). Cleveland Clinic. Retrieved August 18, 2023, from https://my.clevelandclinic.org/health/treatments

/22043-cpap-machine#:~:text=It%20keeps%20yo
ur%20airways%20open

D'Avignon Digestive Health Centre. (n.d.). *Coffee Enemas in Toronto | How do Coffee Enemas work?* Digestivehealthcentre. Retrieved August 20, 2023, from https://www.digestivehealthcentre.com/services-how-do-coffee-enemas-work.html

De Bellefonds, C. (2023, March 21). *Diet for Kidney Health.* EverydayHealth.com. https://www.everydayhealth.com/kidney-diseases/diet-tips-to-help-prevent-or-manage-chronic-kidney-disease/#:~:text=Diet%20Tips%20for%20Kidney%20Health

De Pietro, M. (2022, May 12). *Skin detox: What it is, how it works, and more.* Medicalnewstoday.com. https://www.medicalnewstoday.com/articles/skin-detox#skin-care-tips

DeGrandpre, Z. (2020, May 21). *Is a Colon Cleanse a Good Idea? How Often Should You Do It?* Evidence Based Cleansing. https://cleansejoy.com/is-a-colon-cleanse-a-good-idea-how-often-should-you-do-it/

Diet for a Healthy Liver: Do's and Don'ts. (2022, January 29). Narayana Health Care. https://www.narayanahealth.org/blog/diet-for-a-healthy-liver-dos-and-donts/

Different types of facial treatments & choosing the best facial treatment for you. (2023, March 27). The Aesthetic Skin Clinic. https://www.askinclinic.co.uk/2023/03/27/differ ent-types-of-facial-treatments-choosing-the-best -one-for-you/

Dukowicz, A. C., Lacy, B. E., & Levine, G. M. (2007). Small Intestinal Bacterial Overgrowth. *Gastroenterology & Hepatology*, 3(2), 112–122. https://www.ncbi.nlm.nih.gov/pmc/articles/PMC 3099351/#:~:text=Small%20intestinal%20bacterial %20overgrowth%20(SIBO)%20is%20defined%20as %20the%20presence

Efird, J. T., Anderson, E. J., Jindal, C., Redding, T. S., Thompson, A. D., Press, A. M., Upchurch, J., Williams, C. D., Choi, Y. M., & Suzuki, A. (2022). The Interaction of Vitamin D and Corticosteroids: A Mortality Analysis of 26,508 Veterans Who Tested Positive for SA RS-CoV-2. *International Journal of Environmental Research and Public Health*, 19(1), 447. https://doi.o rg/10.3390/ijerph19010447

Eklund, J. (n.d.). *Lymph System Detox*. Taste for Life. Retrieved August 20, 2023, from https://tasteforlif e.com/supplements/herbs/lymph-system-detox

Elvis, A. M., & Ekta, J. S. (2011). Ozone therapy: A clinical review. *Journal of Natural Science, Biology,* and Medicine, 2(1), 66–70. https://doi.org/10.4103/0976-9668.82319

Eske, J. (2023, January 9). 7 *natural ways to cleanse your lungs*. Medical and health information. https://www.medicalnewstoday.com/articles/324483#ways-to-clear-the-lungs

Fernández-Rodríguez, R., Álvarez-Bueno, C., Martínez-Ortega, I. A., Martínez-Vizcaíno, V., Mesas, A. E., & Notario-Pacheco, B. (2021). Immediate effect of high-intensity exercise on brain-derived neurotrophic factor in healthy young adults: A systematic review and meta-analysis. *Journal of Sport and Health Science*. https://doi.org/10.1016/j.jshs.2021.08.004

Fletcher, J. (2019, February 12). 4-7-8 *breathing: How it works, benefits, and uses*. Medicalnewstoday. https://www.medicalnewstoday.com/articles/324417

Fowler, P. (2009, July 14). *Fatty Liver Disease (Hepatic Steatosis)*. WebMD. https://www.webmd.com/hepatitis/fatty-liver-disease

Friedman, L. (2023, June 20). *Signs Of A Clogged Lymphatic System & 10 Ways To Cleanse It*. Synergy Health Associates. https://synergyhealthassociates.com/cleanse-clogged-lymphatic-system/

5 tips for healthy, glowing skin. (2018a). Mayo Clinic. https://www.mayoclinic.org/healthy-lifestyle/adult-health/in-depth/skin-care/art-20048237

Gagliardi, A., Totino, V., Cacciotti, F., Iebba, V., Neroni, B., Bonfiglio, G., Trancassini, M., Passariello, C., Pantanella, F., & Schippa, S. (2018). Rebuilding the Gut Microbiota Ecosystem. *International Journal of Environmental Research and Public Health*, 15(8), 1679. https://doi.org/10.3390/ijerph15081679

Garg, D. P. (2020, September 18). *12 Amazing Health Benefits of Breathing Exercises! - PharmEasy*. PharmEasy Blog. https://pharmeasy.in/blog/benefits-of-breathing-exercises/

Gilmartin, S. (2023, June 5). *Cupping for Lymphatic Drainage*. MASSAGE Magazine. https://www.massagemag.com/cupping-for-lymphatic-drainage-143039/

Gupta, S., Allen-Vercoe, E., & Petrof, E. O. (2015). Fecal Microbiota transplantation: in Perspective. *Therapeutic Advances in Gastroenterology*, 9(2), 229–239. https://doi.org/10.1177/1756283x15607414

Holly. (2018, December 31). *15 Easy Ways to Stimulate Your Lymphatic System*. Pink Fortitude, LLC. https://pinkfortitude.com/stimulate-your-lymphatic-system/

How You Can Benefit from Happy Chemicals. (2022, July 18). Integrisok. https://integrisok.com/Resources/On-Your-Health/2022/July/Happy-Chemicals

Hughes, D. A., & Norton, R. (2009). Vitamin D and respiratory health. *Clinical and Experimental Immunology*, 158(1), 20–25. https://doi.org/10.1111/j.1365-2249.2009.04001.x

Ion Detox Foot Bath: Benefits & How it Works. (2020, March 12). Rahav Wellness. https://rahavwellness.com/ion-detox-footbath/

Johannes. (2023, February 17). *Is a Sauna Good For Your Lungs?* Infrared-Sauna.co.nz. https://infrared-sauna.co.nz/blog/is-a-sauna-good-for-your-lungs#:~:text=The%20Bottom%20Line%20With%20Infrared%20Saunas%20and%20Lung%20Health&text=Over%20time%2C%20consistent%20sauna%20use

Karama, S. (2022, September 20). *How smoking harms and effects the brain*. Age UK. https://www.ageuk.org.uk/information-advice/health-wellbeing/mind-body/staying-sharp/looking-after-your-thinking-skills/how-smoking-harms-the-brain/#:~:text=We%20found%20that%20smokers%20had

Kourkoumpetis, T. (2022, January 17). 10 *early signs and symptoms of liver disease*.

BSWHealth. https://www.bswhealth.com/blog/1 0-early-signs-and-symptoms-of-liver-disease

La Rosa, S. (2017, June 13). *Limpieza Renal*. Dr. La Rosa. https://www.drlarosa.com/single-post/201 7/06/13/limpieza-renal

Leaky gut syndrome. (2022, April 6). Cleveland Clinic. https://my.clevelandclinic.org/health/disease s/22724-leaky-gut-syndrome

Learn How To Breath - Buteyko Breathing Exercises. (n.d.). Buteyko Clinic. https://buteykoclinic.com/ breathing-exercises/

Leonard, J. (2019, May 28). *10 research-backed ways to improve gut health*. Medicalnewstoday. https://www.medicalnewstoday.com/article s/325293#cleaning-products

Li, L., Gang, X., Wang, J., & Gong, X. (2022). Role of melatonin in respiratory discascs (Rcview). *Experimental and Therapeutic Medicine, 23*(4). https://do i.org/10.3892/etm.2022.11197

Link, C. D. (2021). Is There a Brain Microbiome? *Neuroscience Insights, 16*, 263310552110187. https://doi .org/10.1177/26331055211018709

Liu, L., Qiao, S., Zhuang, L., Xu, S., Chen, L., Lai, Q., & Wang, W. (2021). Choline Intake Correlates with Cognitive Performance among Elder Adults in the

United States. *Behavioural Neurology*, 2021, 1–11. ht
tps://doi.org/10.1155/2021/2962245

Liver problems - Symptoms and causes. (2018). Mayo
C   l   i   n   i   c   .
https://www.mayoclinic.org/diseases-conditions
/liver-problems/symptoms-causes/syc-20374502

Lockett, E. (2021, January 18). *Natural Kidney Cleanse
at Home: Detox Tea, Diet, and More.* Healthline. https://www.healthline.com/health/kidney
-cleanse#foods

Lymphatic system. (2012). Better Health Chan-
nel. https://www.betterhealth.vic.gov.au/health/
conditionsandtreatments/lymphatic-system

Michalak, M., Pierzak, M., Kręcisz, B., & Suliga, E.
(2021). Bioactive Compounds for Skin Health: A Review. *Nutrients*, 13(1), 203. https://doi.org/10.3390
/nu13010203

Möllenhoff,   C.   (2021,   August   6).
*How   to   Do   Shankhaprakshalana   -
Complete   Guide.*   Forceful   Tranquility. https://www.forceful-tranquility.com/how-to
-do-shankhaprakshalana-complete-guide/

MS, A. S. (2020, June 20). *Melatonin—A Powerful Antioxidant for Lung Health.* Nordic.com
. https://www.nordic.com/healthy-science/mela
tonin-a-powerful-lung-antioxidant/

Nall, R. (n.d.). *How to make saline solution at home: Ingredients and uses.* Medicalnewstoday. https://www.medicalnewstoday.com/articles/323842

Office of Dietary Supplements - Choline. (2017). National Institutes of Health. https://ods.od.nih.gov/factsheets/Choline-HealthProfessional/

Patrick, R. P., & Ames, B. N. (2015). Vitamin D and the omega-3 fatty acids control serotonin synthesis and action, part 2: relevance for ADHD, bipolar disorder, schizophrenia, and impulsive behavior. *The FASEB Journal,* 29(6), 2207–2222. https://doi.org/10.1096/fj.14-268342

Pulsipher, C., & Bohin, N. (2016, May 11). *12 of the Best Foods for Kidney Health, Detox, and Cleansing.* Sunwarrior. https://sunwarrior.com/blogs/health-hub/12-of-the-best-foods-for-kidney-health-detox-and-cleansing

Richards, L. (2022, May 26). *Activated charcoal benefits for your skin.* Medicalnewstoday. https://www.medicalnewstoday.com/articles/activated-charcoal-benefits-for-skin

Rivera, W. (2021, June 24). *13 Ways to a Healthy Liver.* American Liver Foundation. https://liverfoundation.org/resource-center/blog/13-ways-to-a-healthy-liver/

Roschel, H., Gualano, B., Ostojic, S. M., & Rawson, E. S. (2021). Creatine Supplementation and Brain Health. *Nutrients*, 13(2), 586. https://doi.org/10.3390/nu13020586

Small intestinal bacterial overgrowth (SIBO) - Symptoms and causes. (2022, January 6). Mayo Clinic. https://www.mayoclinic.org/diseases-conditions/small-intestinal-bacterial-overgrowth/symptoms-causes/syc-20370168

Su, W.-L., Wu, C.-C., Shu-Fang Vivienne Wu, Lee, M.-C., Liao, M.-T., Lu, K.-C., & Cheng Wei Lu. (2022). A Review of the Potential Effects of Melatonin in Compromised Mitochondrial Redox Activities in Elderly Patients With COVID-19. *Frontiers in Nutrition*, 9. https://doi.org/10.3389/fnut.2022.865321

Superti, F., & De Seta, F. (2020). Warding Off Recurrent Yeast and Bacterial Vaginal Infections: Lactoferrin and Lactobacilli. *Microorganisms*, 8(1), 130. https://doi.org/10.3390/microorganisms8010130

Taggar, M. (2023, August 20). *Detox Foot Patches: What You Need To Know*. Holland & Barrett. https://www.hollandandbarrett.com/the-health-hub/conditions/foot-health/detox-foot-pads/

Tash. (2023, March 1). *Liver Cleanse Recipe and How to do a Liver Flush (The Right Way!)*. Holistic

Health Herbalist. https://www.holistichealthherb
alist.com/liver-cleanse-recipe-liver-flush/

Ter Horst, K. W., & Serlie, M. J. (2017). Fructose
Consumption, Lipogenesis, and Non-Alcoholic Fatty Liver Disease. *Nutrients*, 9(9), 981. https://doi.or
g/10.3390/nu9090981

The Healing Power of Hyperbaric Oxygen Therapy.
(2022, September 21). Uhhospitals.org.
https://www.uhhospitals.org/blog/articles/2022
/09/the-healing-power-of-hyperbaric-oxygen-the
rapy

The Healthline Editorial Team. (2018, June 18).
Preventing Digestion Problems. Healthline Me-
dia. https://www.healthline.com/health/digestiv
e-health-maintenance

The Lymphatic System & How To Keep Yours Healthy.
(2019, December 12). Elanora Heights Medical Practice. https://clanoramedical.com.au/the-lymphat
ic-system-how-to-keep-yours-healthy/

*Treatment for Respiratory Illnesses | Ozone
Therapy.* (2021, July 30). Austinozone.com
. https://austinozone.com/education/ozone-ther
apy-treatment-for-respiratory-illness/

10 Benefits of Colon Cleansing. (n.d.). Ga-
iam. https://www.gaiam.com/blogs/discover/1
0-benefits-of-colon-cleansing

10 Signs of an Unhealthy Gut. (2021, July 21). Frederick Health. https://www.frederickhealth.org/news/2021/july /10-signs-of-an-unhealthy-gut/#:~:text=Frequen t%20discomfort%2C%20gas%2C%20bloating%2C

10-step skin detox guide for bright, healthy skin. (2022, June 21). Comfort Zone US. https://us.comfortzoneskin.com/blogs/blog/10-s tep-skin-detox-guide-for-bright-healthy-skin

3 Ways to Boost Lymph Drainage. (n.d.). Rain Organica. Retrieved August 20, 2023, from https://raino rganica.com/blogs/news/lymph-flow

Walters, R. M., Mao, G., Gunn, E. T., & Hornby, S. (2012). Cleansing Formulations That Respect Skin Barrier Integrity. Dermatology Research and Practice, 2012, 1–9. https://doi.org/10.1155/2012/495917

WebMD Editorial Contributors. (n.d.). What to Know About Skin Detoxifying. WebMD. https://www.web md.com/beauty/what-to-know-skin-detoxifying

Whelan, C. (2020, May 11). How to Get Eucalyptus in the Shower: With or Without Branches. Healthline. https://www.healthline.com/health/eucalyp tus-in-shower

White, A. (2018, April 16). How to Do a Natural Colon Cleanse at Home. Healthline Me-

dia. https://www.healthline.com/health/natural
-colon-cleanse#considerations

World Federation of Societies of Anesthesiologists.
(2010, May 17). *The role of the liver in drug metabolism anaesthesia tutorial of the week 179*. WFSA Resource Library. https://resources.wfsahq.org/atot
w/the-role-of-the-liver-in-drug-metabolism/

Younossi, Z. M. (2019). Non-alcoholic fatty liver disease – A global public health perspective. *Journal of Hepatology*, 70(3), 531–544. https://doi.org/10.1016
/j.jhep.2018.10.033

Zhang, C., Hu, Q., Li, S., Dai, F., Qian, W., Hewlings, S., Yan, T., & Wang, Y. (2022). A Magtein®, Magnesium L-Threonate, -Based Formula Improves Brain Cognitive Functions in Healthy Chinese Adults. *Nutrients*, 14(24), 5235. https://doi.org/10.3390/nu14
245235

Zhang, Y., Leung, D. Y. M., & Goleva, E. (2014). Anti-inflammatory and corticosteroid-enhancing actions of vitamin D in monocytes of patients with steroid-resistant and those with steroid-sensitive asthma. *Journal of Allergy and Clinical Immunology*, 133(6), 1744-1752.e1. https://doi.org/10.1016/j.jaci.2
013.12.004